AIDS TO BETTER GARDENING

AIDS TO BETTER GARDENING

Brian Walkden

DAVID & CHARLES : NEWTON ABBOT

0 7153 5341 1

Set in 11 on 13 point Baskerville
and printed in Great Britain
by W J Holman Limited Dawlish
for David & Charles (Holdings) Limited
South Devon House Newton Abbot Devon

Contents

Illustrations

Preface

Gardens are not made without effort. Most gardeners do not begrudge the labour involved because there is a great sense of achievement in doing something creative. But there are, of course, quite a few reluctant gardeners amongst us! A gardening author would be foolish indeed if he supposed that *all* of us enjoy our gardening, especially the regular chores of grass cutting, edging and weeding. Yet no matter which category we fall into, we all welcome equipment that saves us time and labour.

The purpose of my book is twofold. First it suggests or recommends those pieces of equipment which will make life a lot easier for the gardener. Secondly, I hope it will encourage the gardener to take more enjoyment and relaxation in his garden by the construction of leisure sites and the use of leisure furniture.

Inevitably, there are constant changes and developments in garden equipment, and by the page-proof stage of this book three mowers had gone out of production. Textual references to them have been amended accordingly.

Deciding just what to include in my book has been no easy task, but the work has been simplified to a large extent by the fact that I have been able to test a great many of the things I have written about and have constructed many of the features in my own garden—patios, walling and even a swimming pool.

My wife, who is also a very keen gardener, has used a lot of the equipment and her invaluable comments have enabled me to assess it from the woman gardener's point of view.

If my book enables someone to garden with less effort and to find time for more relaxation in the garden, I shall be very pleased. If I manage to convert a reluctant gardener into an enthusiastic one because I have shown him or her the easy way to do things, I shall be absolutely delighted.

Brian Walkden

CHAPTER 1

Cultivating the Soil: Hand Tools

The cultivation of the soil is one of the most important basic garden operations, so naturally there is quite a miscellany of tools to choose from. Selection is made more difficult because there are so many similar tools on the market, differing from each other only in detail. But some of these differences merit attention: it is always worthwhile, for example, to consider the advantages of stainless steel over ordinary surface finishes; and because many cultivation operations are tiring anything in the design which makes for comfort is a good investment.

'Pay a little extra for quality' is sound advice. Tools should be regarded as an investment. Although it is very tempting to buy cheaper tools which look on the surface to be just as good as their more expensive companions, do bear in mind that their years of service will never compare favourably with the better products.

SPADES AND FORKS

Two very important basic tools are the spade and fork. Both can be used for turning over the soil and the fork is especially useful for breaking down large clods when the ground is being prepared for sowing or planting. This is done by hitting the clods with the back of the fork and then giving them a brisk to-and-fro sweeping with the tips of the teeth or tines, as they are sometimes called.

Spades and forks are made in many different sizes (one leading manufacturer lists twenty-seven different spades and twenty-five different forks) but the amateur gardener need only concern himself with two sizes of each. These are the full-size digging spade and fork and the smaller border versions of each. The latter are really delightful to handle, and although they are primarily intended for women, many men have taken to them. The digging spade has a blade of $11\frac{1}{2} \times 7\frac{1}{2}$in, and the border spade a much daintier $9 \times 5\frac{1}{2}$in or even $7 \times 4\frac{1}{2}$in. There is quite a difference in the forks too: the digging version is $12\frac{1}{2} \times 7\frac{1}{2}$in, and the border size is $9 \times 5\frac{1}{2}$in.

The weight of these tools can vary quite a lot and this factor must be considered most carefully when a selection is being made. Too heavy a spade or fork is tiring to use, and the only way to find this out is by handling them in the shop or garden centre. Forget about being self-conscious. Go through the motions of digging and you will quickly discover the weight that suits your personal requirements.

One or two other buying points are worthy of consideration. You need a handle that is comfortable to grip. Moulded or contoured types are the best and many are made from polypropylene, a durable, weatherproof plastic which is warm to the touch in cold weather. D-shaped handles are smooth and fit large or small hands equally well. Strength is vital, so look for tools with solid sockets, where the metal fitting enclosing the wooden shaft is in one piece. The strapped versions which only partly enclose the shaft and are 'split' at the sides are less robust.

Whether the provision of a tread or a thin flat strip of metal on one top half of the blade of the spade adds to the comfort of digging is very debatable. It does reduce the wear on the soles of footwear to a small extent, but it adds slightly to the weight of the tool, and in any case one should always dig in a pair of strong shoes or boots.

The ease with which the fork or spade can be pushed into the soil—especially those heavy, sticky clays—aids work considerably. This is where the stainless steel versions score. There is much less resistance to the soil and the sticky particles do not adhere quite so tenaciously. They are much more expensive of course—usually two or three times as much—but they are a very good investment and, better still, make an ideal present for a keen gardener.

The shape of the teeth, tines or prongs of a fork also affects ease of work. Most garden shops stock the square-pronged type, but there are forks available with streamlined oval prongs which slip through the soil with less resistance.

One special design of great value is the long-handled bedding or border fork, with tubular aluminium handle covered in plastic in its up-to-date version. The 5ft handle is ideal for tilling the soil at the back of wide borders and certainly saves a great deal of stooping.

Garden work has no respect for age or infirmity, when the cultivation of the soil can become quite a problem. The Wolf Terrex is specially designed to help here. It is of metal construction with a special lever and spring arrangement which enables the user to turn over the soil without bending or backache. The head (either spade or fork) of this most useful tool is interchangeable and can be quickly attached. It not only speeds work and reduces effort considerably but can be used by some disabled gardeners also (see page 33).

RAKES

The rake is a real jack-of-all-trades. With it the soil can be broken down into fine particles for seed sowing or planting, areas can be levelled, seed drills taken out and fertilisers worked thoroughly into the surface. Few problems arise in selection. Lightness should be one deciding factor and tubular aluminium handles play an important part in this respect. Plastic sleeving adds to comfort. The number of teeth range from ten to sixteen; the more teeth there are the finer the tilth or soil surface and the more easily it can be prepared, but for general purposes a twelve-toothed rake is suitable.

There are several rakes, known as lawn rakes or lawn combs which are specially designed for the care and maintenance of lawns. They are usually fan-shaped with a span of some 20in and numerous sprung wire teeth in flat or round section. The lawn rake removes dead grass, moss and other debris and is the answer to autumn leaf collection problems. For very fine lawns there is a rake with thirty-three stubby rubber teeth which inflict no damage on the grass.

One of the intriguing features of tool development during the past few years has been the designing of multi-purpose aids to gardening. Many of course have failed to establish themselves for one reason or another but just a few have been welcomed as excellent additions to the general range. A good example is the Tudor Multi-rake which has crescent-shaped tines. The longer tines on the reverse side are used for fine seed-bed preparation and the shorter ones for raking over the lawn (scarifying) or for leaf collection. Rake-head angle is adjustable and the tool is not lifted from the ground during use but pushed to and fro. Its own weight takes much of the effort out of its use. A similar multi-purpose rake is made by Spearwell, but it has only one row of teeth.

HOES

These come in a confusion of shapes and sizes. Basically there are three main types—the Dutch hoe, the draw hoe and the push-pull version—but with many variations in streamlining and contouring. A few unusual models are available and have interesting features to commend them.

Back, however, to the basic designs. The most familiar and popular hoe is undoubtedly the Dutch with its D-shaped blade. The stainless steel designs (and this applies to all three types) with their lightweight handles and contoured hand grips are a delight to use, making light work out of what has to be a regular chore during a very large part of the gardening year. The draw hoe, as its name implies, is used for earthing up or drawing up the soil around plants, and it is invaluable for taking out seed drills, especially wide ones for peas and beans. There are subtle variations in the designs of the neck; the swan-neck version, I find, gives slightly more delicate control. But the most useful hoe is undoubtedly the push-pull design which has cutting edges on both sides of its blade. On the Wolf version the introduction of side-guards enables the user to hoe close to plants without danger of severing them, and it is an admirable tool for closely packed borders. There are some unusual versions with quite pointed serrated edges, but I found these not so comfortable nor so easy to handle, especially in soils with coarse textures.

If you are one of those gardeners who like to get down to it, I recommend the onion or hand hoe. This is a very nice little tool to have and there is a choice of handle length, usually 3–6in.

Many gardening writers extol the virtues of the Canterbury hoe, which is not a hoe but a small three-pronged fork with its head at right angles to the handle and used for breaking down large lumps of soil after winter digging. This is really an unnecessary expense when a fork can do the work more quickly and more effectively. True, it does save bending but it is one of those tools that will spend most of its time rusting away in the garden shed!

PLANTING TOOLS

The design of small hand trowels and forks does not seem to

have progressed a great deal during the past few years. Stainless steel has been introduced to make them easier to use, but on the whole the handles are as uncomfortable as ever they were. However, a new set of aluminium alloy hand tools known as Trigagrip has come onto the market. They have a trigger-like grip on the handles which prevents sore palms, and are ideal for women gardeners.

Graduated planting trowels for bulbs are very useful, especially to the newcomer to gardening who may not be able to gauge planting depths easily. Dibbers are often suggested as planting tools but I find that these tend to compress the planting hole badly, especially in the heavier soils. The roots of a plant must have plenty of room for development and this compression of soil restricts them in the vital early stages and can check growth.

HAND CULTIVATORS

A set of tools that I think are rather overlooked by gardeners are the claw-like cultivators which have a set of curved prongs or tines attached to a 4ft 6in or 5ft handle. Drawn towards the user, these tines cleave through the surface soil and break up the hard 'pan' which so quickly forms, especially after heavy rain or frequent artificial watering. The cultivator is also an excellent tool for working in fertilisers, either as the beds are prepared or when dressings are applied between rows of plants.

Some designs are extremely versatile and have adjustable heads so that from one to five prongs can be quickly attached and up to three rows of small plants cultivated at a time. This tool is very useful in light to medium soils for breaking down large lumps preparatory to final tilth preparation with the rake.

Another intriguing cultivator is a soil miller which consists of a set of star-shaped wheels which provide a working width of some 6in. Equipped with a long handle, it is pushed to and fro over the soil and the teeth of the wheels bite into the soil particles and break them down. A pendulum knife at the rear of this tool controls the depth and also cuts off small weeds at the same time.

LENGTH OF HANDLES

The correct length of long handles is very important and can make all the difference to the comfort of the user. It is unfortunate that very few firms appreciate this; the only one I know of which does provide a choice is Wolf Tools for Garden and Lawn Ltd. They suggest that for a person up to 5ft 2in in height, a 4ft 6in handle is suitable, for a person between 5ft 2in and 5ft 9in, a handle 5ft in length should be selected, and for the gardener over 5ft 9in a 5ft 6in handle is required. These special handles can only be used for the Wolf range of tools, however. But what a nice personal touch it would be if garden sundries firms could offer a tailor-made service like this.

THE MINIMUM NECESSARY

The pocket will nearly always be the deciding factor in the selection of tools where the budget is limited. This being the case it is necessary to select the fewest possible tools to do the maximum amount of work. The rake, for example, used on edge can do the job of a draw hoe in taking out small seed drills; the Dutch hoe can be used at an angle for the same purpose, and a spade will take out flat drills for peas and beans. Soil lumps struck with the back of the spade are broken down nearly as efficiently as with the fork, and the hand trowel does duty satisfactorily for the hand fork.

The minimum collection of hand tools necessary for the basic cultivation of the garden is in fact a spade, rake, Dutch hoe and a hand trowel. The newly married couple could purchase these as a nucleus of their gardening equipment, and gradually add to them as budget allows and interests develop.

TOOLS WITH A DIFFERENCE

From time to time, a manufacturer launches a hand cultivating tool completely different from all the familiar designs. Is it worth buying such curiosities?

Very few of them stand the test of time and usage. Virtually none of the gimmicks which in past years have been sent to me and which I have tested are still around.

Although the gardening fraternity is very slow to accept radical change, it is certainly willing to appreciate sound improvement. If a new idea saves time and effort, then there is a place for it. The Wilkinson's Swoe is a good example of an improved basic tool, the hoe that was given a face-lift. A stainless steel blade of an unusual wedge shape has a handle fixed to one end of it, the handle itself being set at a subtle angle to give pleasant and accurate control.

CHAPTER 2

Mechanical Cultivating Tools

Despite smooth, stainless steel working heads or other good design features, cultivating tools do entail a certain amount of hard and tiring work on the part of users, especially where large areas have to be dealt with. Powered cultivators certainly solve many problems, but they are not necessarily the complete or perfect answer. The virtues of such assistance can be exaggerated, and even more care is required in their selection than in the choosing of hand tools, not only because they involve a much greater expenditure, but also because they are complex pieces of equipment to assess.

There is no doubt that the modern cultivator is a most versatile tool. Many are designed to take ancillary equipment such as grass cutters, hedge trimmers, saws and even air-compressors. There is versatility in size also. They range from models specially designed for the modest garden up to the really powerful brutes for large areas. But despite all their useful features, it is easy to purchase a white elephant! What, for example, do the manufacturers mean when they state that their machine weeds? For inter-row work where the lines of plants are straight or reasonably so, a cultivator will be a tremendous time and labour-saver. But if you think that you can weed between irregularly placed clumps of plants, as in a herbaceous border, then you are in for a great deal of hard, exhausting labour as you struggle to manoeuvre the machine. I have never been convinced that even the smallest of machines is satisfactory for this type of work.

The garden should be planned for the machine rather than the other way about. Fortunately this is not quite as difficult as it sounds because the two sections of the garden which are most suited to powered cultivation operations are the vegetable and fruit gardens. This planning really means the arrangement of rows to suit the working widths of the cultivating heads or tines. For example, one make of cultivator can be equipped with soil rotors or tines which give working widths of from 9½in to 44in. Pairs of rotors can be added as required to provide these widths, a method common to many of the makes. It is a simple matter therefore, to arrange the rows of vegetables or fruit plants to suit these working widths. It is necessary to allow room for turning the machine round at each end of the beds, and a distance approximately twice the length of the machine is usually adequate.

SELECTION CONSIDERATIONS

Selection by the method by which the cultivator works is an important buying consideration. This can be conveniently divided into the following three main groups:

(a) Machines which have an extended arm or boom, at the end of which the cultivating heads are attached, eg the Landmaster Complete Power Gardener.

(b) Machines which have their engine and main frame above the cultivating tines, eg the Wolseley Merry Tiller.

(c) Machines which have their cultivating tines at the rear, eg Howard Rotovators.

Subtle design features now creep into the selection problem. The mode of propulsion needs careful consideration. Many of the cultivators in the small to medium range pull themselves along the ground by means of their revolving tines or rotors. Others have a drive arrangement to their land wheels and are the most stable cultivators to handle whereas several of the other types do take quite a bit of getting used to, especially those that have their engines directly over the cultivating tines. It took me a little time to master the Wolseley machine especially when the minimum number of rotors were used, but once I got the balance right the machine proved to be quite docile. Some designs can have solid pneumatic traction wheels fitted to the rotor drive shaft and a tool bar at the rear of the machine. The machine thus has forward traction from its wheels and complete cultivation equipment at its rear.

The power of a cultivator is related to the amount of work it can be expected to tackle, and the machine purchased should have an engine capacity reasonably in excess of present requirements. For light to medium soils a low powered model would be quite happy, but it would not be suitable for tougher, heavier soils. Usually a 3hp 4-stroke engine is adequate for most garden work. Above this figure the machine is more suited to the professional grower, but those gardens with an acre or more of ground which requires cultivating should consider these 'heavies'.

A few machines are fitted with a reverse drive attachment, a thoroughly useful feature which reduces the amount of turning space required at the ends of the beds, and is therefore much appreciated in the small garden. It need not involve the purchaser in much extra outlay.

I have never understood why some manufacturers do not provide an adjustable handle which can be swung to one side so that the user does not have to walk on the soil which has just been prepared by the machine. Of course it would add to the cost of the machine but it is surely a feature the user would be prepared to pay for. Several machines such as the Farmfitters' Gardencare, models 5000 and 6000, and the Wolseley Professional and Titan designs do have these adjustable handles, and in the case of the Wolseley Major there is a choice of adjustable or fixed handles.

ACCESSORIES

The labour and time-saving virtues of these modern cultivators are further increased by the use of quick-release fittings for the various accessories. Tedious nuts, bolts and spanners have been dispensed with and positive clips or retaining springs are provided. The accessories pose another problem: just what ought one to buy? The manufacturers' catalogues these days are very comprehensive and very well illustrated and provide a great deal of useful information, but making a decision is still far from easy.

A lot depends on the type of soil. If, for example, a really tough hard clay has to be tackled the pick rotors will be a good investment. They are extra strong and specially shaped to bite into the surface. Ordinary cultivating rotors, or slasher rotors as they are sometimes called, are essential for general soil tilling. Special hoe blades are sometimes available and these are designed for near-surface use where they quickly deal with weeds. A set of these would be a useful addition to the accessories.

The larger and more powerful the cultivator, the more substantial the tools or accessories. The big machines are capable of ploughing the soil as well as cultivating it with a rotary action by their tines. Special tool bars or frames are supplied to which tools such as ploughs or furrowers can be attached. Other accessories include multiple hoe blades, cultivating 'feet' or tines, sickle mower attachments and even special cylinder mower units. Many of the machines, both large and small, can have a useful rotary grass-cutting attachment fixed.

One of the most versatile of the cultivators as far as accessories is concerned is the Wolseley Merry Tiller. This range of machine can power the following accessories: a rotary grass cutter, a cylinder mower, a sickle mower, lawn rake, concrete mixer, 5cwt capacity truck, power take-off attachment for saw, hedge trimmer, load carrier, yard scraper, bulldozer (ideal for rough levelling and preparing sites), fertiliser spreader, soil shredder, and air compressor. Obviously, not every garden would require such a formidable array of accessories, but even a small selection of these tools would ensure that most of the routine work around the garden was carried out with the minimum of time and effort.

THE CULTIVATOR IN THE VEGETABLE GARDEN

The advantages of powered cultivators are certainly appreciated in the vegetable garden, especially if a reasonably large area is devoted to the crops. I could not manage my two very large allotments without my small cultivator. The conditions are far from ideal as the ground is on a very steep slope on the side of the Sussex Downs, but even so the machine works well—apart from a little struggling to keep control, which is inevitable in these rather unusual conditions—and its versatility is much appreciated. I find, for example, that I can get much more from my ground in the season. Peas and dwarf beans can be cleared quickly after picking, the beds rapidly tilled and fresh seed put in. It is easy to plan sowings and harvestings for the deep-freeze with far greater accuracy, and bulk sowings and plantings can be carried out with far less effort.

BUYING AND MAINTENANCE

I would certainly not buy a machine unless I had the opportunity of putting it through its paces. No one buys a car on its appearance alone. Various machines handle quite differently and although a particular make may be ideal for the purpose in mind, you may not 'take to it' and would not be happy using it. Moreover subtle differences in weight, length and width may be all-important for your own particular garden layout and requirements. A request to a manufacturer is all that is needed; he will put you in touch with the nearest agent who will arrange a demonstration of a machine or, in most cases, more than one machine, so that you get an idea of their merits. But of course any machine takes a bit of getting used to and due allowances must be made. Do be sure that *you* handle the machine as much as possible and when the salesman makes a point about a particular feature try it for yourself. He may think it good—you may well disagree!

A mechanical tool is only as efficient as its maintenance allows and another advantage of dealing with a local agent is that the machine can be overhauled regularly. There are several garden machine centres around the country where full maintenance and repair services are available. I have never understood the mentality of the many car owners who spend their weekends tinkering about with a perfectly good car—far less do I approve of the owner of a mechanical cultivator attempting to do his own servicing or 'adaptations'. Leave this to the experts who are so familiar with these machines. It will certainly cost less in the long run.

The unusual is the exception rather than the rule in powered cultivator design. One noteworthy design with a difference is the Farmfitters Multigardener. The idea here is to have one power unit as the driving force for different working heads: the 125cc 4-stroke engine can be attached to a cultivator unit, a rotary cutter or a flexible drive unit. This lift-off engine unit provides a versatile power pack and yet is easy to store in the garden shed.

Powered equipment can be a great help to the woman gardener, and in most cases the lighter machines with the least complex fittings and the easiest method of attachment would be a wise choice. The smaller cultivators, particularly those with the boom arm to which various work heads can be fitted, are very suitable. Lifting and weight are cut to the minimum. Controls are few and very simple indeed and the machine in action is as docile as it is possible to make a powered cultivator. Women would find them most useful for hoeing and light tilling of the surface for seed beds, and even hedge trimming becomes enjoyable if a power take-off and flexible drive are used.

I have been very surprised to find that in a few cases manufacturers fail to state the depth to which their machines cultivate. This is a vital piece of information for the would-be purchaser, even though only an approximation can be given. To generalise, most of the machines of 4hp and under till to an approximate depth of 6–12in; the larger machines work slightly deeper, especially if they carry a plough.

Several manufacturers have paid attention to styling. This is a good thing, especially if it means better protection for the engine. It is much easier to clean a machine which is well protected, and a certain amount of streamlining makes the machine easier to manoeuvre. The Honda range of cultivators and tractors are well styled.

PROBLEMS

Problems with powered cultivators are usually associated with the engine itself, and in particular starting it. It is essential that the cultivator be kept in a dry shed with a damp-proof floor: a damp engine will not start easily—if at all! There is nothing to better a strong wooden floor, which is drier than a concrete one, unless a thorough job has been made of damp-proofing the concrete. Oil drips are a slight problem with a wooden floor, but a metal tray or sheet of tough plastic will solve this. Drain the petrol out of the tank if the machine is not to be used for some time. Condensation can form water in the petrol and prevent starting. The plugs must be cleaned occasionally and the air filter examined and cleaned frequently. A great deal of dust is created during cultivation, especially in the summer, and it is surprising to find how far it can penetrate.

My own biggest problem with a cultivator is in keeping the rotors reasonably free when weedy ground is being tackled. Unfortunately the action of the rotors twists the stems very tightly around the shafts and if a mass is allowed to build up it puts a strain on the machine as well as impairing the efficiency of the rotors. I find it a very difficult and quite frustrating exercise! I cannot see, however, how to deal with the problem except to say the obvious, and that is that one should never allow the weeds to grow too tall—but quite often of course a cultivator is being used primarily to clear neglected and therefore weed-grown areas.

CHAPTER 3

Mowing the Lawn

TWO WAYS OF CUTTING

The first thing to appreciate as far as mowers are concerned is that there are two distinct ways in which they can cut the grass. The first is by a rotary action, the second by a revolving or cylinder action. The rotary mower is a very versatile machine because, with very few exceptions, it is the only mower which is capable of dealing equally well with tall grass and with shorter lawn grass. The cylinder mower, on the other hand, is only for the shorter grass which is generally found on ornamental or domestic lawns.

For the finest and best cut, the cylinder mower cannot be beaten. Rotary mowers give a reasonably close and pleasing enough cut but do not produce anything like the fine finish of the cylinder, nor is this in fact claimed by most of the rotary machine manufacturers. Everyone loves those banded effects on the lawn, so much so that several of the rotary mower manufacturers have fitted a rear roller to their machines to provide them (normally a rotary mower does not produce a banded effect). The light rolling of the lawn is also beneficial. Atco's 18in self-propelled rotary, Farmfitter's 16in Lawncare mower and Mountfield's M3 and M5 models all include a rear roller. The rotary cutting action, on the other hand, deals effectively with those 'bents' or pieces of coarse grass which often occur in lawns of poorer quality and so irritatingly survive the passage of the cylinder mower with a front roller.

Some rotary mowers are equipped with grass collection facilities, others not, and the merits or otherwise of grass collection is a subject causing much controversy. The majority of gardeners seem to be rather tidy-minded creatures, especially over their lawns—I have an aquaintance who has even confessed to the use of a vacuum cleaner to deal with some of his mowings!

The argument, or sales talk, that some rotary manufacturers come out with is that grass collection does not matter because their machine cuts the grass so finely that the cuttings are hardly noticeable. In any case, say some, so easy and quick are the new models to use, that you will probably cut the lawn more frequently, with a consequent reduction in the amount of cut grass falling to the ground. This I do not agree with for one moment. Because lawn mowing is so much easier and quicker one tends to do more *other* jobs around the garden and still only mow once a week. In fact, in the average-sized garden mowing is no longer the major task it used to be and many more women now do the mowing for their husbands. Personally, I would always be prepared to pay a little extra for the facility of grass collection—which does also provide me with a lot of valuable compost material. Organised properly, with a wheelbarrow close by, the emptying of the grass box is not such a tedious operation.

The cutting of really tough, tall grass is an entirely different proposition because this work is not done as frequently as lawn mowing, although it is unwise to leave this sort of grass too long otherwise cutting is really hard work. In this case the uncollected grass can be left to rot down and it will act as a mulch. It is a good idea though to rake it off occasionally for composting.

Having decided on the method of cutting he prefers, the gardener has still to make a choice from the wide range of machines available in each group. This is no easy task.

ADJUSTING THE CUTTING HEIGHT

I have always found the easiest mower to use is the one with the fewest possible gimmicks and gadgets, and with its essential controls sensibly placed. High on my priority list is ease of adjusting the cutting height. It is often necessary to make quick re-adjustments, and if the mower has to be run off the lawn to another part of the garden, or back to the garden shed, the cutters have to be cleared off the ground quickly.

Many of the grass cutters with four wheels (the rotaries) have independent height adjustment for each wheel. This is a little tedious compared with the single lever or wheel system which deals with all four wheels at once, but where machines have rollers, the one adjustment is also available. However, a great deal of time is saved on the independent wheel adjustment system by having a lever to each wheel which engages into slots or grooves according to the required height. Independent wheel control has one advantage and that is that lawns along a pathway can be easily cut right over the edge if the two outside wheels are so adjusted that they run on the lower path level whilst the other two wheels run on the grass. This is assuming of course that the location holes coincide with the drop in level and allow the blades to maintain the cut previously set for the lawn.

Height adjustment on hand mowers is usually done by means of a threaded knurled knob which is screwed up or down, or a simple arrangement with a click stop or a plunger which engages with a series of holes. All are quite reliable, but unless the best setting position is marked off in some way it is very difficult to find again once altered. It is also a little difficult to re-set each side in its original position after the manufacturer's setting has been altered. For the small extra cost involved, the incorporation of a positive and visual check would be a vast improvement, and would be specially welcomed by women.

The few continental mowers which are available in Britain cannot be set lower than the British machines and users find that they cannot get the really close cut that many gardeners prefer. I have found that those I have used give a good cut on their lowest setting, although I would have liked to have set about another $\frac{1}{4}$in lower on occasion.

Other features on mowers vary considerably from type to type and, for convenience, I propose to deal with the hand cylinder mower first.

HAND MOWERS

Mower weights

The ease with which a hand mower can be pushed is a very important consideration. Design has improved so much these days that most are remarkably easy. Lightness has a distinct bearing on ease of use and some of the continental designs are remarkably light, perhaps a bit too light on rather uneven lawns. Where there is power to drive the cutters or provide propulsion as well, the weight factor need not be too much of a problem. The Swedish Husqvarna Minor, which weighs 11lb, is a featherweight compared to British light machines such as the Qualcast Superlite Panther at 36lb, the J.P. Mini-Mower at 43lb and the Atco at 41lb. In addition to bouncing about a little on uneven grass these light continental machines also have an occasional tendency to tilt upwards when resistance to cutting is encountered. Nevertheless, they are especially useful for the woman gardener and for the elderly.

Width of cut

Cutting width on hand mowers is another feature which needs careful consideration. For very small lawns, or where there are intricate routes to cut (around flower borders set in the lawn itself), a machine with a narrow cut is useful. The smallest cut is 10in on machines such as the Suffolk Swift, Viceroy Mk

Page 33
The Wolf Terrex, a specially designed spade which reduces effort and is also suitable for the elderly or infirm

Page 34 (*above*) These Wilkinson tools, typical of many modern designs, are finished in stainless steel and have comfortable handles

(*below*) This Wolseley range of cultivators illustrates the versatility of modern designs

II, Webb Whippet, Husqvarna Minor and J.P. Mini-Mower. The most popular cutting width is 12in, and unless the machine is specially geared or light in structure, cutting widths in excess of this figure require much more effort in pushing.

Selection for good finish

The finish to the lawn depends on the number of blades the machine has. This will give so many cuts per yard. The gear ratio determines the number of revolutions the cylinder will make. The popular 12in cut models have 5 blades and these provide between 36 and 39 cuts per yard, a pleasant finish to a lawn though not the best. For a finer finish, a machine with 6 blades will give between 46 and 52 cuts per yard. The Lloyd Pennsylvania (low-wheel) mower, however, is an exception. Despite the fact that this machine has 6 blades, it only gives 41 cuts per yard, but this is because it is designed to cut tall grass—which it does with surprising ease.

The Webb Witch, a 12in machine with 8 blades, is in a class by itself, having 60 cuts to the yard! This gives a most beautiful finish to a lawn and while it revolutionises the look of an ordinary lawn, it really comes into its own (and really should be only purchased for this purpose) where a high quality lawn is made from top quality seed.

The J.P. Maxees were quality machines designed to provide a very fine finish to a lawn with their 52 cuts per yard. An interesting feature of these models is the way in which the complete cutting cylinder can be removed in seconds for re-sharpening. This firm, unfortunately, has recently closed down but there may still be some of these machines around.

Cutting the edges

Hand mowers can be subdivided into two further groups. Those which have rear rollers and those which have side wheels. The limitation with the latter is that they cannot be used over the edges of the lawn, and so their maintenance entails further work with the edging shears. The wide rear roller models can be so guided that they overlap the edge by a few inches to allow the cutting cylinders to operate right up to the very edge. Rear rollers which are ribbed and split are the easiest to use. The ribbing provides a better grip and the split roller ensures easier turning or general manoeuvring in the garden.

It is useful to be able to cut under hanging branches and flowers without getting these entangled or damaged on the mower, and the streamlining on some of the machines helps in this respect. The Ginge Futura, however, has a guard along the front of the blades. It was easy to provide a guard on this particular machine as its cutting cylinder revolves in the opposite way from those on British mowers and throws its cuttings back into a rear-mounted grass box. This is useful in that it enables the user to get right up to a wall or flower borders, which is impossible with a front-mounted box, but the drawback is that if you leave the box off whilst cutting your feet get covered with the mowings.

Grass collection

Check, if possible, the throw of the grass into the box. This could be improved on many machines; some do not throw well at all, and others pile the cuttings up along the edge of the box and seem unable to throw them to the back. Fibreglass boxes would also be an improvement, and would get less badly damaged than the usual metal ones.

Comfort in use

There is a lot to be said for comfortable handles and grips on the machine you propose to buy. It is surprising that manufacturers have not given these details more thought. At least it should be possible to make grips which do not eventually slip off! Grips with some substance to them, with a sponge-like effect, are kinder on the hands. Adjustment for height of handles adds to comfort in use, but on many handles, only a few adjustment positions can be used. Any refinement on this system makes all the difference to the work of pushing a machine.

Cutting tough grass clumps

One of the cutting problems a mower has to deal with is caused by those irritating clumps of tough, coarse grass so prevalent on lawns made from poor quality turves. The front roller usually flattens these and prevents the cylinder from slicing them off. An interesting design feature which is worth keeping an eye open for is front roller adjustment. On some machines, Ransome's Ajax for example, the centre rollers can be removed to cope with these grasses, leaving the two outer ones on so that the mower can still travel.

Of course, where a machine has no front roller, such as the Suffolk Viceroy, Qualcast B1 De-luxe, Ginge and Husqvarna, there is no difficulty in dealing with tough grasses. The Wilkinson Flexa hand machines—rather difficult to come by now as production has stopped—are very effective, and even quite tall, wet grass can be cut extremely well with this machine's unusual flexible blades. The cut it provides on an established lawn is very good also, and it is ideal for giving a newly sown lawn its first careful cut. What a pity, though, that it is such a noisy machine to use!

Finally

The final assessment of any mower is how you yourself get on with it. You can only find this out by a practical trial and if the facilities for this exist through a local dealer or garden centre, do not hesitate to take advantage of them. Ease of movement by the use of good reduction gearing and ball-bearings are particular features which can only be appreciated on actual trial.

BATTERY MOWERS

The introduction of battery motive power was a very important advance in mower design and it has brought many benefits, the chief of which is undoubtedly the ease of starting compared to that of a petrol-driven machine. The battery mower works off 12 volts and is therefore very much safer to use than machines run off mains electricity; added to which, maintenance is considerably reduced.

This extremely simple machine has considerable potential. There is no doubt that remarkable advances in battery design are just around the corner, and the use of powerful miniature batteries or cells will shortly result in much lighter machines and greater cutting duration. At present the battery mower is quite a heavy machine, especially the larger capacity type, and getting it from the shed to the lawn, and up and down steps, is not the easiest of operations. A 12in machine can weigh 90lb and an 18in model some 190lb.

Battery-operated rotaries

An interesting breakthrough in rotary design has resulted from the use of battery power. A 12-volt battery is used as for the cylinder types and of course the main advantage is, again, the easy starting and comparatively quieter running. One design, by Westwood Engineering Ltd, has a 16in blade and 7in diameter wheels which enable it to be pushed into quite tall grass. But there is room for a great deal of development in battery-powered rotaries, and I feel that present-day batteries do not yet provide sufficient power to make this type of mower comparable to the electric or petrol versions. I am sure, however, that it will not be long before a very powerful miniature battery is available which will be ideal for the rotary action.

Noise factor

A battery mower is *not* a silent machine, as one manufacturer has claimed! It cannot even be described as very quiet. No two people agree on noise and noise levels, but it should be appreciated that a certain amount of noise is made by the cutting blades of any mower. Add to that the sound of its engine and the noise level is raised quite a lot. What can be conceded is that the battery machine is less noisy than most petrol mowers, though pretty much on a par with the mains electric types.

Cutting capacity

This is dependent, naturally, on the power in the battery and there is no point in trying to compare it with electric or petrol machines. The recharging of the battery is, however, the simplest of operations as each machine is equipped with a special charger. This is separate from the mower and can sometimes be used to charge the car battery! The unit is plugged into the machine and then into a convenient mains socket using an earthed plug. The charger works on 12 volts and is completely safe. Recharging usually takes 24 hours at an approximate cost of 1p. It is very important to keep the battery well charged, and even in the winter period when the mower is not in use an occasional charge every month maintains it in good condition. It must also be topped up regularly with distilled water, and this, incidentally, can be obtained from the domestic refrigerator when it is defrosted.

As a very approximate guide to duration of use and area capacity, a 12in battery mower will cut for 1hr and deal with 450–700sq yd of grass. A 14in model will run for 1¼hr and cut about 1,000–1,150sq yd, the 14in de luxe version for 2¼–2½hr, covering 2,000sq yd. An 18in model will cut for 1½hr and deal with 2,000sq yd of lawn. These figures refer to lawns where the grass is cut regularly and where the lawn is reasonably level.

The battery mower really comes into its own on the average lawn of about 800–1,000sq yd maximum. There is usually a small reserve of power left and undue strain on the battery is avoided. For larger areas I would prefer to use a petrol-driven machine.

Most of the battery-driven machines give a very good finish to the lawn, with an average of about 76 cuts per yard.

Speed control

Usually two speeds are provided—fast and slow—and a clutch is used to disengage the drive to the rear roller so that the machine can be free-wheeled when necessary, eg in difficult corners. On some of the smaller machines, this clutch control is located in the rear roller. The slow speed is recommended for use in restricted areas and where careful manoeuvring is necessary.

I have always been slightly amused by manufacturers' ideas of what a comfortable walking pace is. There seems to be quite a difference in the speeds provided in various makes and some are quite fast! This is why it is so important to handle a machine yourself before any decision is made to purchase.

Other design features

Grass boxes on the average seem to be of good capacity and the grass throw on most of the machines I have tested is adequate. Many of the designs are attractively styled and the Atco and Webb ranges, which are particularly easy to keep clean, are especially recommended.

ELECTRIC MOWERS

I have used electric mowers of various types for several years in my own garden and all the time I have used them I have never been completely at ease. This is not a criticism of the machines themselves—far from it—but a dissatisfaction with the use of electricity at mains voltage.

Cable problems

There is first of all a certain restriction of mowing freedom simply because there is a mains voltage cable always in close proximity to the mower and more concentration is necessary. Add to this the complications of flower beds in the lawn and other obstacles and the cable becomes a confounded nuisance. However, the electric mower can play an important part in lawn care, especially in smaller gardens where with the 75ft or so of mains cable provided an uncomplicated lawn can be cut with ease. One must just learn, and adhere to, a routine of paying out the cable carefully to one side of the work so that it does not get in the way. One clever answer to the cable problem is a cable drum fixture on the mower which automatically feeds out or rewinds the cable as the mower is used. This is a unique feature of the Wolf VW Cablefix model. Thirty yards of cable are provided, and more can be supplied.

Of course, with a cable extension the electric mower becomes suitable for the larger garden also, and a reel with an extension socket can be used not only for the mower but also for a hedge trimmer.

High safety factor important

One cannot be too careful where electricity is used. Damp or wet conditions and electricity do not mix! Manufacturers of this type of equipment have been very conscious of this fact and have made great efforts to ensure that their machines are as safe as possible. Probably none have done more than Wolf Tools for Garden and Lawn Ltd. Double insulation is provided in all their electric mowers. Only high grade insulation materials capable of withstanding, under severe tests, 5,000 volts are used. Special splash-proof construction, especially for the on/off switch and overload switch on the handles on their Rotondor electric series, protects against moisture and rain.

Cutting systems

Two different cutting systems, rotary and cylinder, are available with electric machines. In the former case machines can collect the cuttings in large-capacity boxes or the grass can be shot out to one side if a deflector plate is used. The Wolf machines mentioned in the previous paragraph are rotary cutters.

Cuts of 12in and 14in can be provided by the cylinder mowers powered by electricity. These are fairly heavy machines weighing 94–100lb, according to width of cut. It is good to see that the Webb company can provide machines with stepped-down voltages via a separate mid-earth transformer. The voltage is reduced from 200/250V AC to 110V AC.

Development in the reduction of mains voltage for the electric mower in the garden is highly desirable. It is a costly business at present but surely a compact and realistically priced unit could, with determination, be made available. There is, understandably and reasonably, a general fear of using electricity in the garden, and anything which can make the use of electricity there absolutely safe will be a tremendous advance. Manufacturers would sell more machines and gardening labours could be considerably reduced.

PETROL-DRIVEN MOWERS

Starting

Whenever I come to use my motor mower I always wonder whether it is going to start the first time! I must admit that I have been pleasantly surprised to find that, on most occasions, the engine fires successfully at the second or third pull. I put this down to having my mower (in fact, all my equipment) in a nice dry shed which has a good wooden floor. Dampness is the enemy of an engine, particularly of the electrical parts, and most starting frustrations arise from keeping the machine in a damp place.

But dampness is not the only enemy. Dirty engines, particularly the plug, carburettor and air-filter, can cause poor starting. Faulty ignition timing, dirty magnet points and even a blocked exhaust silencer also give a great deal of trouble. I wonder, too, how many people fail to check the fuel level and try to start an engine with an empty tank? It is all too easy to do. I know because I've done it myself! And where the mower is not used in the winter months, the petrol tank should be drained to prevent condensation forming in the tank. If this occurs you will not be able to start the engine.

Improvement in engine design has done much to ensure better starting and reasonably quiet running. The latter consideration is very important and some manufacturers have fitted their machines with special silencers. Motor mowers used in built-up areas where there is considerable echo and amplification of noise via the walls of buildings can prove a little troublesome; there is a case here for investigating the merits of electric or battery-operated machines.

Whilst on the subject of starting, I thoroughly recommend the impulse starter as the easiest method of starting a mower or any other petrol-engined piece of equipment. This consists of a handle which, on being wound round and round, winds up a powerful spring. Depress a lever or button and the spring unwinds and kicks the motor into life. This is a lot easier than the recoil starter which entails the winding of a length of tough cord around a pulley wheel fixed to the engine in such a way that when the end is pulled smartly the wheel is turned and the engine fired. Unfortunately, only the higher priced machines are at present fitted with the impulse device. Some of the large and expensive ride-on mowers are fitted with an electric push-button starter, just like a car. This is real sophistication!

Cutting and controls

The choice of cut is, as in the electric types, either rotary or cylinder. There is virtually no cutting problem which cannot be solved by the petrol-driven mower, and one distinct advantage with this type of propulsion is that there is no limit to the area which can be cut. Golf-courses, paddocks, orchards etc can all be dealt with most efficiently.

Machines range from those with a modest 12in cut to the large gang mower, towed by a tractor, with a cutting width of 20ft or so. For the average gardener the 12in and 14in cutting widths are adequate. Anything larger than this becomes too uneconomical price-wise. For the lawn of half an acre and upwards the 17in and 20in machines are ideal and cover the ground with surprising ease.

The 'ride-as-you-mow' type of mower is well worth considering for large areas. These have 24in cuts and a special detachable seat arrangement so that you can also use the pedestrian version of the machine when you want to. The seat is set over a wide roller and a special linkage system allows for very close turning around flower beds and corners of the lawn. This new coupling system is one of the big recent improvements in design; these machines can now turn in their own width.

Examples of these machines are the Atco Riding Mower and the Webb Ride-on. The latter has an electric push button start in one of its higher-priced versions. It is essential to select a ride-on which has a foot brake if it has to cope with downhill gradients, or the machine will get out of hand. Very fine finishes can be obtained with both these machines. The Webb, for example, gives 80 cuts to the yard.

Controls on petrol machines are very similar to those on electric and battery-operated models. A clutch engages or disengages the drive to the roller so that the machine can be freewheeled whenever necessary. Most models have a special engine-speed governor which ensures that the engine never labours when the going is tough.

I like to see a ribbed rubber covering for the split rear-rollers of cylinder mowers. I find this gives a lot more traction or grip, especially if the lawn is slightly damp when the grass is cut. This feature also ensures that the machine is quiet in use, and when it is being taken from the shed to the lawn. Vee-belt drives are also quieter than the chain version. Both these features can be found in the Hayter Ambassador 16in and 20in mowers.

EXCEPTIONALLY FINE CUTTING

There are gardeners who take especial pride in their lawns: their grass is of the highest quality and beautifully fine. This type of lawn demands a mower of equal merit, one that will give a very close, fine, velvet-like finish. There are a few machines specially designed for this purpose and they are used mainly for the cutting of such fine grass surfaces as bowling greens and golf greens.

The Toro Greenmaster is one such machine, providing an amazing 147 cuts per yard! It is a very expensive piece of equipment, of course, because it contains so many unusual and important features. One of these is a free-floating cutting unit which follows the contours of the ground very closely and eliminates scalping. The machine actually consists of three separate units: the cutting unit, the tractor or engine unit, and the catcher support unit which is a rigid frame, integral with the tractor unit, holding the grass box or catcher. The cutting cylinder has 9 blades and a 21in cutting width.

Another out-of-the-ordinary machine—but again no more of these are being made, due to closure—is the J.P. Super Mk5B 24in model which has an instantly detachable cutter unit. The standard unit is provided with 5 blades, but there are 3 and 7 bladed units available. This makes it a most versatile mower. The 3 bladed cylinder cuts rough grass; the 5 blades give a good, standard finish and the 7 blades provide a really fine finish at 78 cuts per yard. The rear roller is made in three sections to give quite exceptionally good turning facilities.

JEEP-LIKE MOWING

For the real fun of lawn cutting, the miniature tractor or jeep-like machines cannot be bettered. These cut by a rotary action and are ideal for large lawn areas, be they rough or smooth. They are, in fact more like cars to drive than mowers, with their automatic gear change and speeds of about 5-8mph. The motors are very powerful of course, in the region of 6hp. Miniature tyres on the wheels add to the comfort of the user and cuts of 32in width soon deal with large grass areas.

Close cutting without scalping, or with only very little on very rough terrain, is provided by the floating-type cutter unit which is slung underneath the chassis. For the large garden or estate these machines are especially useful because when the mower unit is raised well off the ground they are transformed into miniature tractors capable of towing accessories such as trailers, lawn spikes, leaf sweepers and fertiliser distributors. Some of the more expensive designs are equipped with electric starting.

UNUSUAL DESIGNS

Among the many mowers available, two deserve special mention, not only because they do a good job of work, but because they are so novel in design. The first is a machine called the Flymo which works on the hovercraft principle and floats just above the ground as it cuts the grass with its rotary cutters. There are two types available, a petrol-engined version and one run off mains electricity. Widths of cut vary from 15in to 21in, the smallest cut being that of the electric version.

I found these machines refreshingly easy to use, because

they simply floated along. Weight problem is completely overcome except when the machines have to be carried to and from the lawns. This, I think is a drawback to the range, especially if the shed is some way away from the lawn. The machines are reasonably light at around 28lb, but all the same carrying them is rather tedious and the rather large handles can be a nuisance in restricted areas.

I was disappointed with the cut the electric version gave one of my lawns when I had the opportunity to test this machine: on the other hand, I have heard enthusiastic reports from other users. The lawn I used it on was not of particularly good quality, having been laid some years previously from turf, and in rather a hurry. I would have expected, however, a better closer cut. On the closest setting there was a lot of scalping but this setting did produce a slightly better finish.

The hover mower really comes into its own when used on slopes and banks. It is the only machine that can cope with the contour problem. Really steep banks can be cut if the machine is fastened to a length of strong rope by its handles and put into a very careful, slow pendulum action by the user standing firmly at the top of the bank—work that is best carried out on a firm *dry* footing.

Rough and tall grass presents no problems to the Flymo range, and the Contractor model is specially designed for large tough areas of grass as well as for large formal sites.

The second machine, the Brott, is very unusual in appearance and its method of cutting especially intriguing. A series of cutting flails set in three banks swing loosely on the fins of a fast rotating balanced rotor. These fins create a draught which blows the cuttings into the large collecting sack at the rear of the machine. This mower cuts a section 20in wide, and is a self-propelled ride-on machine with the operator sitting right at the front with a wonderful view of the work ahead.

It is a machine for the really large lawn, whether the grass be rough or fine. Three forward speeds and a reverse gear make the machine extremely easy to handle in spite of its rather clumsy appearance. When it first came on to the market it had several faults—the grass chute particularly was rather unsatisfactory in those early days—but all these have been remedied in the latest designs.

BASIC CARE OF LAWNMOWERS

The service one gets from a mower depends on the care with which one looks after it. It is all a matter of a little common sense. Moving parts, particularly the spindles, gear wheels, chains, axles etc must run freely and effortlessly or the mower will be difficult to handle, especially if it has to be pushed. Freely running parts place less strain on a motor too, and this is especially important for battery-powered machines as undue strain quickly drains the battery power. Under no circumstances should dirt be allowed to cake on these moving parts; they should always be wiped or brushed clear after use. Perhaps some enterprising manufacturer will provide a neat kit of cleaning tools with his machine one of these days—a small, thin brush among them please!

Always have a can of oil handy so that these moving parts can be given a small amount regularly. Do read the instructions which are supplied with each mower and familiarise yourself with the various oiling points. I find aerosol sprays excellent for oiling and also for giving a thin protective coating of oil all over the metal parts of my mowers. Some parts of a mower are rather difficult to get to with the oil can but the forceful spray of the aerosol penetrates every time.

Some of the paint aerosols are very useful too. Like many other gardeners, I always manage to scrape the mower somewhere—especially the grass box—but a quick retouching with an aerosol paint prevents rust.

The rollers of a mower must always be cleaned after use. Uneven rollers cause poor cutting, and a roller with dried soil or stones on its surface can seriously damage a fine close-cut lawn.

It is surprising what continual vibration can do, especially if the mower has to be taken to the lawn along a hard pathway, so check regularly that screws and bolts are firmly in place.

Always keep a mower in a dry shed—preferably one with a wooden floor. Dampness quickly causes rusting, not to speak of starting problems with petrol mowers.

One of the most important maintenance tasks is the sharpening and setting of the blades and this should be done before the new cutting season commences. Send the machine to a local specialist firm; there are do-it-yourself sharpening aids available but if sharpening is to last the season it is a task for the expert—so is the setting of the cutting blades with the bottom plate. At this time of year a motorised machine should also be given a thorough overhaul with special regard to the engine. Most leading manufacturers have accredited local agents and they should provide the best service. Not only will they be fully acquainted with the make but will have a range of spares too.

SAFETY

Particular care is needed in the use of a motorised machine, especially those powered by mains electricity. Frequent examination of the cable for defects such as cuts, cracks or natural deterioration is vital. A fault on a mains cable can be lethal. Make sure that connections are sound, especially where the cable enters a plug. *Waterproof* cable connections *must* always be used and under no circumstances should you use cheap accessories. Use only what is specially designed for the job; the manufacturers themselves usually supply all that is necessary.

Always disconnect the mower from the mains when attending to it, and make sure when you have to adjust a petrol mower that the motor is switched off. This may seem very basic and obvious advice but it is surprising just how careless many gardeners are.

Keep young children away from motorised mowers and never leave a running engine unattended. The lawn should be examined before a cut is given, and especially before the first cut of the season, so that stones etc can be removed. This is especially important when a rotary machine is used because the blades can eject objects at considerable force.

Page 51 (*above*) A Webb petrol-powered cylinder ride-on mower

) The Concorde, a
:er mains electric
r by Qualcast is light
ıdle and ideal for
oman gardener

Page 52 (*above*) Jeep-like mowing is great fun. This Allen ride-on mower soon deals with large areas

(*left*) The lightweig
Ginge hand mower

CHAPTER 4

Lawn Care

EDGING

A lawn is as neat as its edges. Lawn edge trimming is a most important finishing touch to the lawn but it can be very tiring and tedious work without the proper equipment. The lawn edge is maintained neatly in two distinct operations: the edge itself needs to be cut out cleanly and defined by the use of an edging iron, and afterwards the grass has to be kept within bounds along this edge by frequent cutting with an appropriate tool such as a pair of shears or some other mechanical device.

For very small areas, the hand shear is probably the best tool to use. The work is tiring enough on the wrists but is soon done. Long-handled types do away with stooping and bending, and provided the mower can be taken over the edges of the lawn edging shears with a vertical cut only need be used. Where this is not possible (ie if you used a side-wheel mower) some of the grass near the edge will have to be cut horizontally either with a pair of ordinary shears or the long-handled, horizontal-cut model. There is nothing to equal the one-handed shears for cutting the grass in awkward corners and edges.

A very useful innovation is the grass catcher 'tray' which can be fitted to the bottom blade of a long-handled shear. As the tray fills up it can be emptied on to the lawn as work

D

proceeds, and when all the edges have been trimmed the lawn itself is mowed and these trimmings collected by the mower.

For larger lawns, the more sophisticated edging tools designed for speedy work are desirable. Push-along types are the cheapest and several good designs are available. Most of these work on the same principle: they are equipped with a land roller or wheel which, when pushed over the lawn, turns a special cutter at the side of the tool. The wheel or roller is carefully guided along the edge of the lawn and the cutting wheel trims off the overhanging grass quickly and neatly. One of the best of these has a ribbed metal roller which is tapered slightly, and a T-handle provides a good grip and ensures excellent control. The manufacturers of this excellent Atco tool do not publicise it enough! Another design of edger has an egg-shaped rubber roller which makes it easy to alter the angle of cut, simply by twisting the edger over slightly to left or right.

The easiest and fastest way of all to trim the lawn edges is by the use of battery-operated edgers. They are real gluttons for work, and on one charge one of these can deal with about a mile of lawn edge. They are generally powered by a 12 volt battery and equipped with chargers.

Successful and rapid edge trimming depends on the maintenance of a clean, well-defined edge to the lawn and it is necessary to cut out this edge occasionally with an edging iron. The depth of the edge is important otherwise the blades of the edging tool will catch on the soil or path below. Most edgers can negotiate irregular outlines quite well but sharp bends should be avoided when making a lawn in the first place.

There is another way in which the edge of the lawn can be kept well defined. This is by the use of aluminium or plastic strips. These are inserted along the face of the lawn edge and close up against the soil. The lawn should first be cut out cleanly with the edging iron and the strip then carefully tapped into place so that its bottom edge bites into the soil border. The top edge of the strip should be *just* below the level of the lawn so that the mower can be taken right over the top without catching the edging strip. The green or natural coloured lawn edging is less obtrusive than the aluminium finish, especially when used in round or oval borders set within a lawn or along the drive. Of course, it is all a matter of personal taste but it is probably best that this type of garden aid should be concealed as much as possible.

There is one rather unusual lawn edging tool which is manipulated by hand. It is very similar to a pair of long handled shears except that the blades can be positioned at several angles through an angle of 90°, that is from horizontal trimming to vertical operation. The blades are operated by a trigger on the handle and the complete tool is pushed along on wheels. I found this edger very handy for small jobs but rather tiring on the hand and fingers when a large amount of trimming was required.

AERATION

What makes a good lawn? Many factors are involved, such as good soil preparation, adequate drainage and regular feeding and weeding, but one of the most important requirements is aeration, and many gardeners seem to be ignorant of this fact. Unless the grass roots can 'breathe' easily, they will not grow vigorously and their condition will be reflected in the poor quality and coverage of the grass itself.

Is it really so surprising that the surface soil in the lawn becomes hard and compacted considering the heavy wear and tear it receives during the season? This pan prevents air from entering and a lot of water simply runs off and fails to penetrate. Fertilisers also fail to reach the grass roots. The surface, therefore must be kept open, or aerated, and this is where special tools help. Spikes or aerators are available in many forms and sizes to suit all types of lawns and areas of grass.

The deeper the penetration the better, but this has its snags because the deeper the penetration the greater the effort required. Hand spiking can be a very tiring operation and only the garden fork is really capable of going down to any great depth. It should be driven into the grass every 12in: on a small lawn this is hard work; on a large lawn it is quite exhausting. A compromise has to be made, and spiking to a depth of about 2in is usually considered adequate. In the hand aerator range there are three types of tool made to effect this penetration. The first is a hollow-tine fork or tool that takes out a core of soil which is ejected into a collecting box on the tool. This type of aeration is the best in my opinion because the holes can be filled in with sharp sand afterwards (the sand is scattered over the lawn surface and then worked in with a stiff brush or the back of a rake) and a system of miniature drains is formed with the sand helping to keep the holes open. A motorised version of this hollow tine system provides a penetration of 4in and a working capacity of some 1,200sq yd per hour.

There are several solid-tine aerators, some in the form of a hand fork, others much more sophisticated. One version is provided with wheels so that as the machine is pushed along the lawn the spring-action lines bite into the ground to an approximate depth of $1\frac{1}{2}$in. About 150 penetrations per square yard are provided, and models are available in 9in or 12in widths. My chief criticism of this type of aerator is that it is quite noisy in use and a little tiring too, though of course one cannot expect hand-operated lawn aerators to be the easiest things to push around.

Another push-along design has a series of star or spur-like aerators which slit the lawn surface as they run over the ground. A platform is provided over them so that penetration depth can be increased by placing bricks on it as required. Rather a crude system, yet an effective one.

The most complete range of lawn aeration equipment is

provided by the Sisis company. Models range from simple hand-operated tools to tractor-drawn models specially designed for large areas such as sports grounds. This firm is one of the few who have appreciated the need to provide three different types of tines for various times of the year. For the spring and autumn, flat slitting with wedge-shaped blades ensures that fertilisers and dressings enter the soil efficiently: piercing before and after application is the best system to adopt. In the summer, round pointed solid tines provide moisture penetration, drainage and entry of air. Hollow tines are used in the late autumn to overcome compacted surface soil.

The most labour-saving method of aeration as far as the amateur is concerned is to let your motorised lawn mower do all the work for you! Special Mow-Rite aerators can be fitted quite quickly to the rear of most makes and you can then aerate as you mow. These aerators are star-shaped wheels fixed in a simple metal framing. They can be left on the mower and disengaged simply by pulling a lever fitted to the owner's handle bars. It is important to state the make of mower when ordering this equipment.

WEEDING AND FERTILISING

For the small lawn hand application of fertiliser and weed-killer is the best method to adopt. It is not, of course a very accurate system, but accuracy grows with experience. Marking out the lawn into yard-wide strips with pegs and line gives a reasonable guide.

But for the larger lawn mechanical fertiliser and weed-killer distributors are real time and labour-savers (and also for the vegetable garden if the surface soil is reasonably fine and level) and ideal tools for women gardeners. They are very easy to set or regulate and the job is just like pushing a pram around the lawn!

There are not many of these machines about and it is wise

to purchase the more expensive models which provide the most accurate distribution. There are three of these, the Sisis Truspread, the Sisis Super Coultas and the Andrews Cyclone. The first two spread the materials by means of a moving conveyor belt driven from the ground wheels. No matter what the operating speed, the application rate remains constant. The Super Coultas model in particular is a very accurate machine especially designed for professional use and for high quality grass such as bowling greens. A unique feature of this model is the circular brush which spreads the material over the ground and is very handy for the clinging types of fertilisers. Application rates of ½–2oz per sq yd can be set.

The Andrews Cyclone applies its dressings in quite a different manner, virtually broadcasting the material by its spinning rotor. What I particularly like about this machine is its ability to spread up to 6ft in width, which makes it a very useful time-saver. About 120sq yd per minute can be dealt with and the machine has a wide application rate of from 4oz to 3lb per sq ft. The application is not quite as even as with the other machines, but for general garden purposes it's a jolly good investment.

CHAPTER 5

Pruning and Trimming

SECATEURS

Why manufacturers keep turning out so many almost identical pruners, I cannot understand. It simply adds to the customer's confusion and there are seldom any significant differences in design. All that is wanted from a pruner is a pair of sharp hard-wearing blades, an action which reduces the cutting effort, and a comfortable handle or grip. Lightness and a good balance are other factors worth considering, and there should be size and weight differences, particularly in the interests of the woman gardener.

Flower-gatherers

There is no point in buying special flower-gatherers. A small, lightweight pair of secateurs will suffice, strong enough to do all the general light pruning yet handy enough for flowers. Cut-and-hold secateurs are moderately useful for gathering blooms but the natural instinct is to use both hands, one to hold the flower stem and the other the secateurs, especially if the flower is difficult to get to.

Designs have certainly improved over recent years. Styling is given more thought and handles are contoured and plastic-covered for greater comfort. Regulation of the opening of some blades in two or three positions makes secateurs quite a versatile piece of equipment where different thickness or toughness of wood is dealt with. This facility also enables the user to adjust according to the size of the hands.

The larger and heavier secateurs can be quite tiring to hold after a short time, especially if the user is reaching up into branches. Strong, lightweight alloys are overcoming this problem in some designs.

Type of cut

Many people are confused by the way in which secateurs cut. Some models have a flat bottom blade or anvil and the top blade cuts down on this. Others cut like scissors. There are a few designs which cut with a sliding action and these tend to give the cleanest cut over the longest period. The Rolcut secateur range has a good sliding action, the off-centre pivot causing the blade to be drawn down along the anvil while cutting. Another good feature of this range is the availability of interchangeable replacement parts such as blades, springs and rivets.

The Felco range of pruners have an even more complete replacement service, virtually every part being on the supply list. It is also one of the few secateurs which can be provided with a special locking-catch for left-hand pruning. That's attention to detail for you! Quite a revolutionary design idea has been introduced in a Felco model and that is the rotating handle. This has one handle which is much thicker than the other and it revolves around its own axis and allows normal hand movement. A much better grip/power ratio is attained and it is one of the few pruners that can be used for long periods without strain. This is an important point because nothing tires the muscles of the arms more than a pruner which is not comfortable to use. The constant opening and shutting action required places a strain on the wrist especially and as the work becomes progressively more tiring the care with which one prunes lessens.

Selection according to plants

The selection of secateurs must be guided by the types of plant in the garden which require pruning, and particularly the toughness and thickness of their branches. Obviously thick branches of large fruit trees or shrubs cannot be tackled with the smaller hand pruners.

In most gardens a general-purpose type will do what is required. Some manufacturers name them as such. This pruner is midway between the small lightweight models and the large heavier designs. The woman gardener will not find them uncomfortable to use. But better still are two pruners—a small lightweight pair and a medium to heavy-duty type; for the larger gardens where there is usually a much greater variety of plants the two will probably be necessary.

Long-handle pruners

There are occasions where it is necessary to prune branches which are out of reach of the ordinary hand pruners, even when the user is standing on a ladder. In this situation, special long-arm or long-reach models will be required.

A handle length of 6ft may not at first seem long enough, but when you add the height of the user also, a very useful reach is obtained; add to this the height of the ladder and this length of long-arm pruner should be adequate for most gardens. If necessary, pruners can be purchased with handle lengths of 8, 10, 12 and 14ft. In most designs, the cutting blades in the head are operated by a cable via a lever at the bottom of the long handle.

One long-arm pruner can be converted into a long-handle pruning saw. The saw blade is quickly attached to the top of the handle and is capable of dealing with fairly tough branches. The saw's teeth are set to bite on the downward stroke to facilitate cutting.

Although these long-arm pruners can cut toughish wood

it should be appreciated that they are really designed for general light trimming or thinning out. Usually, cutting capacity is only up to a maximum of about $1\frac{1}{4}$in.

For tough cutting

In really tough thick wood a saw will have to be used on branches needing to be cut out (page 66). But for the cutting of moderately thick branches within easy reach, there are several heavy-duty tree pruners or loppers available. The cutting action and power is transmitted by a specially designed lever movement of the handle and cutting blades. I have used these types quite often in my own garden and I am always amazed at the ease with which the powerful jaws bite through the wood. The action is nearly as effortless as cutting through thin branches with ordinary hand pruners.

Blades

Many secateurs are made with hollow-ground blades. These are the sharpest and seem to keep their edge or keenness for a much longer period than ordinary blades. The only problem is that they cannot be re-sharpened easily by the gardener, but this can be undertaken by approved agents.

Several manufacturers provide specially finished or coated blades which resist rust. These certainly keep in excellent condition for a long time but unless they receive sensible home-maintenance such as a good cleaning and light oiling after use, the surface does tend to stain.

KNIVES

In a chapter on pruning and trimming, I suppose mention should be made of special pruning knives. I do so half-heartedly, because I do not think that the average amateur gardener will find this type of knife so useful or so efficient as a pair of secateurs. In the hands of a skilled, professional gardener it is quite a different proposition, but I myself am never really comfortable with a pruning knife and find that I can get on much more quickly with my secateurs. One of the main problems with a knife is that it is not easy to maintain the very keen cutting edge which is so necessary for good accurate work. Very few people can put a keen edge on a blade—and keep it there.

Of course, for work such as budding or taking cuttings a knife is very useful, and for budding it is the only suitable tool. Pruning knives have a curved blade which 'pulls' into the wood as it is drawn down on it: the budding knife, on the other hand, usually has a straight edge to its blade and a slanting tip. The handle of the budding knife is tapered at its end so that it can be inserted in the cut to open up the bark for receiving the bud.

SHEARS AND TRIMMERS

Keeping plants neat and in good shape is not only a task for secateurs. Shears play an important part in this routine work and are especially useful for hedge trimming. Lawn edges too can be kept neat with the hand shear.

The gardener is provided with quite a range of different models from which to choose, and weight, balance and general comfort are bound to be decisive factors, though the type of wood the shears will have to deal with must be taken into account. It is wise to select the lightest pair of shears possible if a lot of hedging has to be cut—if the hedges are tall, you would appreciate a heavy pair even less!

Some of the lightweight designs are very efficient in cutting, especially if they have hollow-ground blades, or blades with a wavy edge which are excellent for tackling tall grasses. Contoured and plastic covered handles combine good looks with increased comfort, and some designs (even in the larger shears) are provided with cushioning in the bottom of the handles so that the jar experienced in opening and shutting is reduced to the absolute minimum.

Avoid cheap shears

A method by which blades can be tensioned by a special locking device is an excellent feature on shears, because at some time or another blades tend to loosen and open up, and once this happens the cut is seriously impaired. Avoid cheap shears where this fault is bound to occur quickly. Cheap shears are also unsatisfactory in that handles easily come adrift: the metal part is usually only wedge-fitted into the end of the wooden handle and this works loose either through use or if the wood becomes wet. On the more expensive shears the handle is generally an integral moulding or casting.

One-handed models

These are very useful for dealing with awkward grass corners and any other places where it is difficult to get the mower. In my garden I use them around a man-hole cover and under several large cone-shaped plant containers. They are quite tiring however for any large-scale work. Women gardeners find the one-handed shear ideal for the quick trim here and there on the lawn and my wife uses a pair for cutting down the dead tops of border plants, but they are not intended for dealing with tough growth.

POWERED TRIMMERS

Electric and battery power has been harnessed for trimmers and has proved a tremendous boon to those gardeners who have extensive hedges. But particular care is necessary in the selection of a powered hedge trimmer because they are surprisingly heavy pieces of equipment to handle. I have been dismayed on several occasions to find that some I have tried out are quite tiring, especially on tall hedging. Supporting and controlling a heavy trimmer is quite an exhausting experience I can assure you!

Of course, some weight is unavoidable because of the motor unit. Balance is perhaps the most important buying point to observe—a relatively heavy trimmer can be much more comfortable to use if the balance is right. If your hedges are tough, your choice must lie with the heavy-duty machines which can cut growth of about $\frac{11}{16}$in diameter, and these weigh something in the region of 10lb. The lighter machines, at around 4lb, have a useful cut of about $\frac{3}{8}$in diameter and this means that they are ideal for most popular soft wood hedges such as privet.

Ease of handling depends a good deal on the design of the handles. There are so many different kinds that it is not possible to detail them here, and it would not be profitable to try because the hedge trimmer is one of those garden tools that absolutely must be handled in the shop. One type of handle, good though the design may be, may not suit any one particular individual. The type I find very useful is virtually a semi-circle. This enables me to hold the tool at any angle with the maximum comfort and safety.

Safety is of vital importance with these mechanical cutters and especially so with the electrical models. The cable *must* be kept well away from the cutters; one way of ensuring this is to make a habit of slinging the cable over your shoulder while you work. Always make sure that the cable is examined regularly for wear or cracks and see that the cable connections are sound. It is unwise to cut wet or damp hedges with an electric trimmer.

Battery-operated hedge trimmers, by contrast, have the advantage of complete safety, working as they do on a mere 12 volts. The use of a battery also dispenses with the need for external mains electric power points or long expensive leads where hedges are some way from the house. Although only about an hour's efficient cutting is available from a full charge, a great deal of hedge can be trimmed in that time. If there is a slight drawback to a battery trimmer, it is that its limitation of cutting to one hour per full charge is perhaps not enough in the very large garden.

Solving distance problems

One answer to the problem of hedge cutting at a distance from the house could be the use of a special flexible drive shaft coupled to a power unit such as a motor mower or cultivator. Another is to purchase a miniature portable petrol motor to which the tool can be connected, the Tarpen Mini-engine, for example, which weighs only 7lb. An independent power unit which can be wheeled to the site and to which the cutting tool can be attached via a flexible drive is yet another solution. There are petrol engines or portable generators available, and although they are expensive items at around £60 or £70 they may well be worth it. A generator, the Andrews Jenny for example, is particularly versatile as it can provide power for accessories such as drills, lighting and saws, as well as hedge trimmers.

SAWS

There is probably a very limited use for this type of tool in the average garden, and even in the very large garden or estate it will be used only infrequently. There is no question, however, that this is the tool for cutting down trees or offending large branches. For these purposes, heavy-duty models are necessary and this is where the powered saw comes into its own.

So well have these been designed that the new user quickly learns to handle them in quite difficult situations, even high up in a tree. And when a tree has been felled the powered saw swiftly deals with the situation by cutting the trunk up into manageable logs. The ease with which the saw rips through the wood is most satisfying.

The chain saw, as it is called, can be powered either by electricity or by a small built-in petrol engine; both are noisy, the petrol engine version especially. The cutting chain is covered by a guard, but even so the greatest care is necessary when this type of tool is used and under no circumstances should children be able to get near it.

CHAPTER 6

Artificial Rain

Although the English summer is subjected to considerable ridicule, supplementary summer water is still needed in the English garden. Under glass, the problem becomes more acute because intense heat is built up and the rain is kept out.

Few gardeners have any idea of the amount of water which is required to thoroughly soak the soil. Who would realise, for example, that half an inch of rain falling over an area of some 500sq ft represents about 650 gallons of water! I wonder how many gardeners now wonder whether their water applications are sufficient!

So many people think that just because the surface soil of a pot or border looks dark after a watering that that is sufficient. If they were to stir the top half-inch or so, they would probably find it quite dry underneath. The secret of success with watering is to apply plenty over a reasonably prolonged period.

Watering can become a time-consuming task, especially in the large garden, and needlessly so. With a little thought and organisation a simple yet efficient watering arrangement can be set up in any average-sized garden. It is not an expensive matter. Much of the equipment is uncomplicated, very modestly priced, and should give many years of trouble-free service. In fact push-button watering for the whole garden is a reality these days!

HOSEPIPES

The basic requirement for a satisfactory watering system is the hosepipe and let me state here and now that cheap hosepipe should be avoided at all costs. Not only will it kink badly and become quite untameable, but its thin walls will not enable watertight unions to be made with the hose connections. A strong hosepipe is easier to handle and will withstand a great deal of wear and tear.

The longevity of hose depends on the way it is stored and the only proper way to do this is on a hose reel. The cheapest consists of a strong wire framework, which usually takes about 120ft of pipe. When this frame is fitted to a stand it is a very simple matter to spin the reel round either to unwind or wind up the hose.

I would like to persuade the reader to invest in a more expensive hose reel, either the type that can be mounted on a wall or the side of the shed, or the type that is mounted on a small wheeled cart. Both kinds have a through-feed system, which means that the water passes from the tap, through the axis of the reel and into the hose itself. Once connected to an outlet socket and to the mains water tap, any length of hose can be unwound and used whilst the water passes through it.

The Wolf hose reel takes up to 200ft of $\frac{1}{2}$in hose or about 100ft of $\frac{3}{4}$in hose. The Hasel models accommodate 120ft and 200ft of $\frac{1}{2}$in hose, but unless the Hasel type is carefully sited it can be difficult to draw off the hose, especially round corners. For convenience I prefer the reel on a cart when it can be taken more easily to the site especially in a complicated garden layout.

Hose connections

Nothing is more annoying than a hose union which leaks, resulting in loss of water pressure and reduced efficiency in an attachment such as a sprinkler. One of the worst problems is the connection to the tap itself if this is not threaded. Design of tap connections is poor generally, with very few exceptions, and accessories for hoses such as on/off connections aggravate the situation because the sudden shut-off of the water supply in the hosepipe can blow the hose off the tap unless the fixture is a very good one. The Hozelock and Gardena tap connections are the best I have used, and do not cause any damage to the tap either. They are fitted very quickly and will withstand shut-off pressure.

The linking together of lengths of hose again requires secure fittings which, if necessary, can be disconnected in the minimum of time. Snap-on types are now available to which accessories such as sprinklers can be attached. These also make the hose a more versatile piece of gardening equipment because on/off valves and Y-pieces enable the user to make up quite complex watering layouts. All these fittings are for the standard $\frac{1}{2}$in plastic hose.

PERMANENT LAYOUTS

There is a lot to be said for a permanent watering system in a garden. This, I find, cannot be decided upon in a hurry. It takes about three months of general watering in the garden before all requirements are appreciated and positions determined. The awkward corners which are not easy to water, and the places where a tree or structure may stand in the way of a sprinkler, so causing a small section of ground to be missed, should be noted.

The instalment of a permanent watering system can be carried out by anyone who is reasonably handy; certainly no plumbing expertise is necessary. The materials used are all strong plastics and the pipe itself is made from frost-proof $\frac{1}{2} \times \frac{3}{4}$in polyoric alkathene tube. It can be cut easily with a sharp knife and all joints are of the push and screw-on compression type.

The main idea is to bury the pipe a few inches under the ground (this is most easily done along the edges of soil borders) and, where required, to join standpipes to it of the same material, about a foot or so high. Special T-joints are used for this purpose, the main pipe being cut and the two ends connected to the two ends of the T-union, and at the top of each standpipe a plastic tap or hose connection is fitted. In this way points for the hosepipe can be made available in any part of the garden. Only a short length of hose (12–15ft) with a sprinkler need be connected to any one of several standpipes. In large gardens branch lines constructed from the main pipe will reduce the length of hosepipe needed; these also are connected by means of T-joints. L-shaped unions are used where the main supply pipe has to be taken round corners or round obstacles in the layout.

Obviously, it is as well to conceal a watering system as much as possible, especially in the ornamental parts of the garden, and the standpipes should be kept to the minimum, both in length and numbers. If a good sprinkler is selected, the number of hose connection points needed in the average large garden is about six and perhaps two or three in smaller gardens, depending on layout of course. The system can be connected permanently to the house mains and regulated by a stop valve which is also available in alkathene. An alternative is to connect to a suitably placed tap via a length of ordinary hosepipe, but in this case, to comply with regulations, it is necessary to disconnect the hose after each watering. This is because water boards feel that there is a risk of suck-back of contaminated water into the mains where a water system is buried or at ground level.

Pop-up watering

For the larger garden a more sophisticated automatic system is certainly well worth considering. This also uses alkathene tubing which is connected to a series of suitably placed pop-up sprinkler heads. These, as their name implies, pop-up above their 'golf-hole' in lawn and border when the water is turned on. In the resting position, the heads are slightly below ground level and the mower can be taken right over those set in the lawn.

Linked to a control panel and hydraulic valves, various sections of the garden can be watered in turn automatically on a time-switch system. One distinct advantage of this arrangement is that the garden can be watered at night when water pressures are usually at their best. It also does away with the inconvenience of drawing off water from the domestic supply during the daytime.

These pop-up sprinkler heads are very powerful and in many cases it is only necessary to install them at 60ft intervals. Adjustments are possible on the heads themselves so that full, half and quarter circles of watering can be arranged.

SPRINKLERS

Oscillating

This type of watering device is becoming increasingly popular and deservedly so because it is a versatile, simple, and relatively inexpensive piece of equipment.

An oscillating sprinkler has a central spray bar fitted with numerous nozzles through which powerful jets of water are emitted. The bar itself moves from side to side, and in this way a large area of ground can be watered at any one time.

The travel or movement of the bar can be controlled or set to provide a number of different watering arcs. The usual settings are full, left throw or right throw from the vertical, and slightly left and right from the vertical. Any one of these combinations, with the sprinkler carefully sited, will cover most watering requirements in the garden and very good control of water delivery is possible. In some front gardens there is often a low wall alongside the pavement, and very difficult it is when using a sprinkler not to wet the pavement and passers-by as well as the garden. But with the oscillating sprinkler this problem is easily overcome as it can be placed practically alongside the wall and set so that it throws its water from the vertical, forward into the garden and away from the wall. Even this arrangement would fail of course if there were a strong enough wind blowing in the opposite direction.

Coverage is usually controlled by setting a dial on the sprinkler to the particular area required. These are marked as rectangles, a rather unusual shape for watering but most useful for lawns, flower beds and vegetable rows.

Coverage varies of course according to the size of the sprinkler but typical areas dealt with are: 32 × 50ft (1,600sq ft), 40 × 50ft (2,000sq ft), 30 × 60ft (1,800sq ft), and 40 × 60ft (2,400 sq ft).

Another type of oscillating sprinkler is used for large-scale commercial watering. This takes the form of a series of spray lines positioned on stands above ground level with a mechanical oscillator fixed to one end of each spray line and connected to the water supply. The oscillator turns the line from one side to the other through an angle of more than 100°. An irrigation width in excess of 50ft is achieved and a 100yd sprayline can apply about ¼in of water in one hour (at a water pressure of 35/40lb per sq in).

Revolving sprinklers

Circular watering patterns are provided by these and they are particularly useful in smaller gardens. Areas of 20–50ft in diameter are provided for.

The revolving sprinklers, like the oscillating types, have feet or skids so that they can be drawn to another watering site by pulling on the hose. I find this only practical along a long stretch of lawn or border, and usually it is necessary to turn the water off before the sprinkler can be repositioned.

The revolving arms are fitted with adjustable nozzles so that the water pattern can be altered and the trajectory varied. It takes a little time to become expert in this setting procedure especially when also trying to adjust the rate of flow via the tap! Usually, however, one finds that a particular setting of the nozzles is sufficient for most purposes and the regulation of the tap itself is quickly mastered by counting turns.

Unless a revolving sprinkler has a high trajectory, tall plants, in the herbaceous border for example, tend to form a barrier and prevent the water from reaching others beyond. For this reason I prefer to use the oscillating type which has a high throw, making the droplets fall more like natural rain. Carefully positioned, however, the revolving sprinkler does do a good job of watering and as I do not want to be dogmatic I recommend the reader to study the growth of plants in his own garden before making a decision on which sprinkler to buy.

The reciprocating sprinkler

This is also a revolving type but works on a reciprocating or 'flip-flap' system, as one manufacturer so aptly calls it. It is most fascinating, if a little noisy! Briefly, the water supply strikes a special spring-loaded plate or arm which is flung back by the force of water. This in turn strikes a part of the turret head and turns the head round slightly. The combined action of water and sprung arm produces a continuous 'knocking' movement which jogs the watering head round. Once the head reaches the stop position it returns right back to its original position and begins to move slowly round again to the stop. This stop can be altered so that the travel of the rotating head can be stopped at any desired position.

Quite a coarse application of water is provided in the form of broken water droplets. Good surface penetration is achieved. Some of these models are fitted to a 3ft metal stand or spike and are to be recommended for watering amongst tall or straggly plants. From a suitable position in a border, the water is carried over most of the growth and finds its way satisfactorily to the soil below.

OTHER WATERING DEVICES

One method of watering I am particularly fond of is mist watering. As its name implies, a very fine mist-like drift of water is applied to plants, outdoors as well as under glass where it is perhaps better known and more often used. Greenhouse mist watering will be discussed in a later chapter.

Outdoors these special spray heads can be fitted to stands 3–4ft above ground level, to provide a wonderful 'dew-type' moisture. I find this type of watering ideal for young delicate seedlings and plants in a frame or in the seed beds. The soil is soaked without becoming hard or panned and no damage is caused to foliage. The system can be installed as a permanent layout in beds or borders and especially in the rockery where this gentle watering will seek out every nook and cranny. The only drawback to mist watering is that it is affected by winds and tends to be blown off course as it were.

Still on the subject of fine water application, the perforated or irrigation hose is well worth looking at. This is a specially designed hosepipe, available in lengths of 20 and 30ft, with hundreds of tiny perforations along its top half and these produce a very fine mist-like spread of water over quite a wide area on either side of the hose. This hose is ideal for watering young seedlings as the water will not beat them down. Quite low water pressures will produce a very good application.

WATERING CANS

Although the hosepipe and various types of sprinkler will supply most artificial watering requirements, the watering can should be regarded as of equal importance, especially if frames and a greenhouse are established in the garden. It is a convenient method of carrying and applying water and invaluable for outdoor spot watering of window boxes and plant containers. For indoor watering these cans are essential and the popularity of indoor and house plants has brought them to the fore as important items of gardening equipment.

Watering cans are available in quite a wide range of sizes or capacities. Miniature designs are a must for indoors, both because water requirements are not large when regular attention is paid to the watering of indoor plants, and because it is much more convenient to get at room plants with a small can. The small spout also assists considerably in control of water direction and flow.

Many cans are attractive in material, line or decoration and an embellishment to the house, particularly those made from copper. Water capacities are usually in the regions of 1–2 pints.

For the greenhouse, capacities must be greater and there is a very sensible range of sizes. Cans in the medium range hold 3, 4, 6 and 8 quarts and the larger models have capacities of 1, 1½, 2, 2½ and 3 gallons. Materials are usually either metal or plastic, the latter producing a lighter and brighter can in gay colours. There is a lot to be said for brightening up one's gardening! It pays to buy plastic cans from well known manufacturers such as Haws or Geeco where top quality is assured. This is not to say that other makes do not give useful service but I do find that the better known makes are stronger on the whole, especially in handle fixings and spout assembly.

Most cans are sold with one or more rose heads, giving a choice of fine and coarse watering. For greenhouse work especially it is essential that the rose can deliver a very fine application when required, for seed boxes or pans and for any stage of growth where plants are delicate. Some of the most accurate fine roses are made from brass, but there are several quite reliable plastic versions on the market.

A medium to coarse rose is essential also for watering mature plants both in the greenhouse and outdoors. A few of these are made with a brass rose and plastic body, and designed to fit most makes of can of ½–2½ gallon capacity.

If money can be spared a special can should be set aside for weedkiller application. Even though plastic cans are a little easier to clean than the metal ones, and are very definitely less susceptible to corrosive products, it is always wise to keep one can only for weedkiller work. There is then no possible danger of contaminating plants.

When fitted with a special spray bar, the watering can becomes a very efficient weedkiller applicator. The spray or weed bar, as it is sometimes called, is simply a short length of small hose plastic or metal tubing with perforations. It is fixed at right angles to an arm which is push-fitted into the spout of the watering can. Some quite short weed bars are available which are very handy for getting in between closely spaced plants in the border.

CHAPTER 7

Carrying

WHEELBARROWS

I am always surprised to find that so many gardeners manage without a wheelbarrow! I could not do without mine. Perhaps people just fail to appreciate how useful such a piece of equipment is, and how much time and labour it can save.

I know of several cases where a wheelbarrow has been purchased and yet is seldom used. This is generally because it has been bought in haste and is not suitable for the job. More often than not it is too large or heavy. Like all tools and pieces of equipment, care is necessary in its selection.

Strength, lightness and balance are the most important factors to consider, and in that order. Modern designs meet the first two requirements but unfortunately not always the third.

One wheel or two? This can pose a problem, but for the woman gardener the choice everytime should be for two. This provides manoeuvrability combined with good control. Balance is usually very good too. For the elderly person this type of wheelbarrow is excellent and places the minimum strain on the user.

Comfortable use is assured if pneumatic tyres are fitted to the wheelbarrow. A wide tread assists in the control as well as providing ample cushioning effects on rough ground. Nylon bearings and axles also ensure smooth action with minimum maintenance.

Special features

Several designs have rather intriguing features. Some have detachable bodies and these are usually found on the two-wheel designs. This is a useful feature as the load can be lifted off and emptied anywhere and the chassis can be used as a truck for the transportation of heavy sacks etc.

Small tool racks or trays can be clipped on to the bodywork of some and this means that small hand tools, gloves, twine and so on are always on hand when the wheelbarrow is in use.

One or two designs have strong, flexible polythene bodies (most are of heavily galvanised steel), combining strength with lightness. These are capable of holding water so are invaluable as temporary storage tanks when the watering can is in use. Fertilisers do not affect this type of material either.

The capacity of a wheelbarrow is an important consideration. The smaller ones usually hold approximately 3cu ft. Larger ones hold about 4cu ft. Capacity can be increased substantially (almost doubled) if an extension top is used for the transport of light, bulky materials such as lawn mowings —it certainly reduces the trips to the compost heap!

Most wheelbarrows are left outside because they do take up quite a bit of room in the shed. One model, the Timperley Fold-A–Kart, can be folded completely and stored flat against the side of the shed; even the two wheels fold away. It is the ideal truck for the woman gardener.

The ultimate in wheelbarrows is the hover-pallet, which is virtually a floating platform some 8ft long and 4ft wide. A powerful fan driven by a 136cc 4-cycle petrol engine floats this pallet over any sort of terrain with a full payload of about 300lb. The frictionless movement reduces effort to practically nil; all the user has to do is to guide it. This is certainly an excellent example of things to come although it is obviously more suited to the commercial gardener.

THE GARDEN BASKET

Carrying on a much smaller scale is an essential exercise in the garden, so we must not forget the small garden basket. Two types are available and both are called trugs. The main difference between them is the material used in their construction. The traditional trug, or Sussex trug as it is affectionately known, is made from wood and is a beautiful piece of craftsmanship. The other type is made from plastic and is usually quite gaily coloured in reds, or greens.

For gathering of produce, collection of weeds or dead flower heads, the trug is indispensable. It is quickly emptied into the barrow close by if a lot of weed gathering is necessary. It is, of course the ideal gardening accessory for a woman.

CHAPTER 8

What's its Name?

One of the most infuriating things that can happen to a gardener is to forget what he has sown or what his new plant is called! This should never occur if labelling is properly carried out—but how easy it is to say this! Labelling, however, must be a matter of strict discipline especially during the very busy seed-sowing periods both indoors and out.

Short cuts to labelling such as marking the sides of the pots or scribbling on the seed box or pan should be avoided at all costs. Those marks are soon smudged or obliterated by handling and watering. There is really no excuse for not having a few labels handy. They are very cheap and long-lasting because the modern label is made of plastic or aluminium. There are wooden labels also but the metal or plastic ones are better.

PLASTIC LABELS

Plastic labels are available in several sizes and shapes. This is necessary because they have to be used in different parts of the garden and for various sizes and types of plant.

The simplest kind is used for the marking of seed boxes, pots and outdoor seed beds. Individual labelling of outdoor plants such as annuals and herbaceous plants can be done with these too. Sizes are many: the smaller ones are about $\frac{1}{2}$–$\frac{3}{4}$in wide and 3–4in long; the larger sizes are usually $\frac{3}{4}$in wide and 4–6in in length. White is usual but it is possible to obtain green or even black labels. For clarity I prefer the white ones.

Satisfactory labelling depends on the durability of the inscription. This has only to last a short time in the case of seed boxes, pots and outdoor seed beds but permanent marking is essential for permanent plants. For short term purposes special pencils can be used and the writing removed with detergent or warm, soapy water when necessary. Labels can be reused in this way for many years. For permanent inscriptions, special inks are available in white or black, with suitable pens to apply them. Fine-tipped felt pens are also very useful for this type of work.

There seems to be a slight difference of opinion about the correct way of writing a label. Should the wording start at the top and run down, or start at the centre and run up? The most sensible method is to place the label down on the table or staging with its point towards the right. Write down the plant details, starting as close to the top end as possible making sure that the wording etc does not extend much into the bottom half of the label. This ensures that should the bottom part of the label get broken off, there will still be sufficient wordage left to identify the plant.

Labels mounted on stems are particularly useful for outdoor work and for the labelling of permanent plants, especially in the border. A much larger writing surface is available which is necessary if plants are to be identified as one walks around the garden. Several sizes are available for these also; a typical example is a $3\frac{1}{2} \times 2$in writing area mounted on a plastic stem some 9in long. For alpines in the rockery labels are correspondingly smaller, usually 3×1in on a 6in stem. For the popular greenhouse alpines even smaller labels are required, say $1\frac{3}{4} \times \frac{3}{4}$in mounted on a $3\frac{3}{4}$in stem.

There is a lot to be said for a labelling system where the height of the label 'grows' with the plants. One such extending design in galvanised wire is 24in long and will extend to a maximum length of 42in, the label being gripped or wedged in the top loop. There is also a range of non-extending wire label-holders which are 24in high.

METAL LABELS

Lightweight, alloy labels are most durable and extremely neat in appearance. Special inks are available for writing on these labels. Some labels have a specially treated surface so that a pencil can be used. Lengths of 4, 5 and 6in are the most popular sizes. One useful feature about some of those is that they have a stem which can be twisted carefully around a cane or even the plant itself. Many of them have a hole at one end so that they can be tied to a plant or support very quickly and easily (this applies also to wood and plastic labels).

A LABELLING MACHINE

One of the quickest ways of labelling neatly and very clearly is by the use of a special labelling machine. To make the label, you dial a wheel to spell out the required words or numbers. Whenever the trigger is pressed the words or letters are embossed on a vinyl tape. When completed the required length of tape is cut off by pressure on a button. As this tape has an adhesive back it can then be quickly fixed to any clean, smooth surface.

Tapes of $\frac{1}{4}$ and $\frac{3}{8}$in widths can be used on different machines; about 40 labels, 3in long, can be produced from a 10ft reel of $\frac{3}{4}$in tape. This works out at less than 1p per label.

I have found this device particularly useful for labelling in the shed. Tool drawers can have their contents marked clearly and a very tidy and orderly shed can be maintained. Very neat labels can be produced for plants in the garden, and for trees and shrubs in particular a branch-encircling label can be quickly made up if one end is inserted into a slit or hole in the label after it has been placed around a suitable branch.

For labelling seed boxes and pots I think this method would be a little expensive because most labels have to be rewritten each season when new varieties are used and sowing dates are changed. For permanent marking they are much more economical and useful.

Finally, no matter what type of label is used, it is important that the correct information is written upon it. This should include the plant's name and variety. When seed is sown, the sowing date should be noted. This latter point is important as the progress of various plants can be recorded for future reference, especially if greenhouse temperatures are being experimented with.

Page 85

(*right*) Rapid lawn aeration is a feature of this Sisis tool

(*below*) Leaf sweepers like this Wolf model will save a lot of time in the autumn

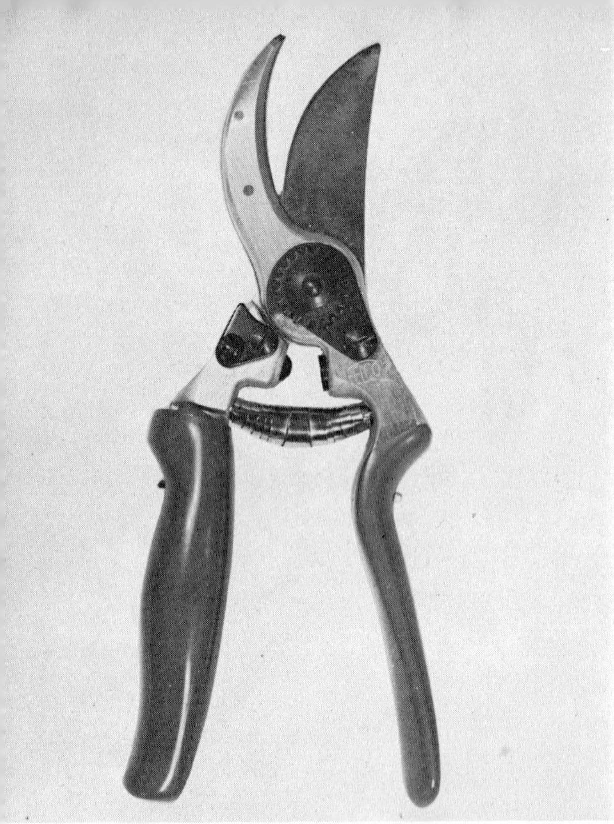

Page 86
(*left*) Precision secateurs ensure a keen cutting actic and these Felco models can be quickly taken to pieces for maintenance

(*below*) Tough pruning requires equally tough too like these special heavy-duty Rolcut loppers

CHAPTER 9

Training and Support

Good training has three advantages—it encourages better growth, it enhances display, and it enables the gardener to look after the plants more easily.

Thoughts on training should really commence *before* a plant is put in. If this is not done—and how often this is the case—it can be quite difficult to provide this training when the plant has become well established—and very likely out of control!

I am referring, of course, mainly to those plants which are trained against a wall or fence. The modern plant support or trainer is in itself quite an attractive affair and does in fact considerably enhance the wall or fence it covers even before it is finally clothed by the climbing or trailing plant.

Most plant supports take the form of either very strong rigid plastic mesh extrusions, or wire or metal rods clothed in plastic or nylon. The great virtue of both kinds is that they give completely maintenance-free service. They never rot or need replacing, which is more than can be said for the old-fashioned wooden trellis or wire supports.

PLASTIC MESH

The square rigid mesh design which provides firm plant support has several good features. The training and tying in of the plants is considerably simplified as the mesh sizes are quite large—4in and 6in. The plastic surface reduces the danger of damage to tender growth by chafing during windy weather. Colours are attractive too, generally green, black and white. If complete eventual concealment of training material is desired the green is the best to use.

The plastic mesh type of support is available in mesh sizes of $\frac{1}{2}$, $\frac{3}{4}$ and 2in. Although immensely strong, it can be cut easily with scissors and is therefore very easy to manage. I have found this particular type of netting ideal for clothing posts and pillars with plants. A roll can be cut to length, wrapped round the post and fixed in place. This makes an ideal support for a climbing plant which eventually conceals the netting.

The plastic support materials can be fixed quite easily to walls or fences. One of the easiest ways is to hang the netting on galvanised hooks. Make sure though that it is suitably supported along its sides to prevent sag: plants are quite heavy, especially after rain or snow.

Another simple method of fixing is to use vine eyes which can be screwed or driven into the wall or fence—both types are available. The mesh is then fixed to these eyes by wire. Always use either galvanised or plastic covered wire for this purpose. The wire is weatherproof and there will be no danger of it breaking later on.

CEDARWOOD AND DEAL

I appreciate that there is a great feeling for wood among gardeners and that many still insist on using this material for training and supporting. But the only type of wood I would recommend is one which has a natural resistance to rot. This is cedarwood. It has a beautiful warm brown colouring which gradually weathers to a silver-grey, but the wood does not lose its wonderful anti-rot properties.

Ready-made panels can be purchased from horticultural

sundriesmen. For decorative purposes a fan-shape is useful, most units being about 6ft high. Widths vary but a useful size is one which is about 18in wide at the base spreading out to some 36in at the top. Square panels are more usual. Most of these are 6ft high and 3–6ft wide. As cedarwood is a comparatively weak timber it is wise to select panels constructed from fairly thick timber sections. Nothing under $1 \times \frac{1}{4}$in should be considered.

Cedarwood is much more expensive than other softwoods such as imported deal. Where cost has to be kept down the deal types can be used but initial treatment with a preservative is vital. Once erected the panels are virtually impossible to treat satisfactorily. Creosote is an excellent preservative but not the best for support and training frames because it may scorch the tender growth; it takes quite a long time before newly treated timber can be considered safe. I prefer to use copper naphenate, which is sold under a proprietary name such as Cuprinol. The green or horticultural grade should always be used. The preparation soaks through the wood very quickly and dries out just as rapidly. Particular attention should be paid to joints and sawn ends.

COATED STEEL ROD

One of the latest ideas in plant supports or trainers is a framework of 8swg welded steel rod. This is completely sealed with polythene in attractive colours and is absolutely weatherproof.

The method of fixing allows a gap between panel and wall or fence of about $1\frac{1}{4}$in. This not only facilitates tying and training but it ensures movement of air behind the plants and greatly reduces the danger of mildew forming in damp, close weather conditions.

Panels work out quite economically because it is not always necessary to cover a wall completely with them to provide adequate support. They can be spaced well apart and the climbing or rambling plant trained to grow and spread from one to another.

There is a very decorative fan-shaped trainer available in $\frac{1}{4}$in steel rod with a tough PVC coating. It comes in a simple do-it-yourself pack which slots together very quickly to make a 6ft high support with a span of about 4ft at the top. Several units can be used together to form arcs or complete semi-circles. I find this type of unit very satisfactory for supporting plants on either side of doorways or porches.

Gardeners would do well to consider this type of trainer, and the squared units previously mentioned, for patio or terrace features where supports for plants so often detract from the attractive appearance of screen walling. They are easily fixed to the mortar courses in the stonework, and blend well with surrounding features. They could for example be used as links between separate wall sections to provide concealment while giving an air of spaciousness. Being completely weatherproof they are maintenance free and, of course, quite strong.

If outlay allows, several of the square or oblong units can be used as a fence or division in the garden, though they need to be supported at intervals by suitable wooden posts to which they are fixed. They might well solve several problems in front gardens which have low retaining or boundary walls, where they would form an effective barrier to animals and young children and at the same time provide an attractive support for plants.

ARCHWAYS

Archways or pergolas are ideal for making the fullest possible use of climbing or trailing plants.

The old-fashioned wooden rustic arch is still very popular and probably suited to an 'old-world' garden layout. But these do eventually deteriorate and become a nuisance and even dangerous. If they are stained and varnished after the bark has been removed they will last a little longer. But there are no problems at all with plastic-coated metal arches. One type has a diamond mesh pattern in an attractive green colour; another and more sophisticated model is made of tubular metal with a nylon coating and looks particularly pleasant in a modern garden layout.

When purchasing an archway of any type always make sure that there will be ample headroom when the structure is in position. Allow for the foliage that you intend to train over it. The height should be at least 6ft 6in or better still 7ft.

INDOOR TRAINING AND SUPPORT

The popularity of house or indoor plants has brought with it a fascinating collection of essential accessories, and among them various forms of plant support.

The problems that face the householder with indoor plants are to find a simple method of providing support or training without detracting visually from the plants and to do this without damaging the decor. There are a few good products which foot the bill admirably.

An excellent way of displaying house plants is to fit to the wall a metal framework on which pots can be fixed. There are several nylon or plastic-covered units for this purpose, each with a number of pot holders and a choice of several positions for them.

The plastic-coated square mesh metal panels mentioned on page 90 can be brought indoors too and used as room dividers with plants trained up them.

One of the most intriguing devices I have come across is a sort of spring pole, attractively finished, which is fitted between the floor and ceiling. The powerful spring holds the pole rigidly in position and the four plant-pot holders provided can be located at any position on the pole. The range of adjustment enables the pole to be used in any room with ceiling heights between 7ft 6in and 8ft 6in, and it is quite simple and quick to move from one position to another. House plants of a trailing habit are ideal for this type of display unit and a veritable cascade of foliage can be achieved as the plants mature.

Plants in a greenhouse are not such a problem because the methods used for training and support are not selected for eye-appeal. For tomatoes and similar crops strong training wires are fastened to each end of the greenhouse; and to these, cane sticks or strong twine can be fixed as supports. For spreading crops such as cucumbers and melons it is advisable to provide a framework, eg several horizontal strands of wire spaced about 1ft apart, or plastic mesh netting suspended from horizontal roof wires at a position half way down the sides of the greenhouse and about 1ft above the soil level.

CHAPTER 10

Stop the Birds!

There seem to be two distinct schools of thought where birds are concerned. Some gardeners like to encourage them because they are such interesting and amusing characters. Others do their utmost to keep them away.

There is no doubt that many birds are a nuisance in one way or another but the damage they do over the season is very small. Pigeons are probably the worst offenders and blue tits can damage buds. Damage is often related to weather conditions: during prolonged dry periods succulent vegetable crops such as peas are attacked, and probably for their moisture. Dry hard weather makes it difficult for birds to bite into the hard pan of the soil and so they turn their attention to soft crops.

Most bird damage occurs in the fruit garden and it is here that the gardener should consider some form of protection, according to the type of fruit being grown. It is relatively easy to throw netting over low-growing strawberries but tall plants such as the currants require more thought.

NETTING

Various types of net are available for fruit protection. The cheapest is repaired fish net—quite a good buy if you are prepared to replace it every few years. Cotton netting is also available but this tends to tear badly and has a short life.

For durability, nylon and ulstron should be considered. These are very tough materials and should give many seasons of good service. An even tougher and more weather resistant material is bitumenised terylene, and the toughest of all is mesh of 100 per cent high-density polythene. One very considerable advantage of this last material is that it does not tangle. Although it is very malleable, it has a certain rigidity in its mesh and is therefore extremely easy to handle in large sheets.

One important point to bear in mind when netting is being ordered is that in the case of diamond mesh the specified dimensions relate to the net as it is bought, ie with closed mesh. When the net is in use and spread open for protection it loses approximately one-third in length and width. Square netting fully covers the area specified.

Mesh sizes should be considered carefully. It is surprising how small a mesh some of the very small birds can get through! The $\frac{1}{4}$in mesh is the one to go for if you want protection against tits, for example; other sizes are $\frac{1}{2}$, $\frac{3}{4}$, 1in and 2in, and for pigeons and other large birds there is a 4in mesh available. An advantage with this size is that it is not damaged by snow; even a light fall exerts considerable weight on a close roof netting.

FRAMEWORK

To be effective, a net should be supported clear of the plants it is protecting. Birds are very cunning creatures, and blackbirds and thrushes have been known to jump up and down on top of netting to get at the fruits underneath! Although netting over the tops of plants does much to deter birds it only needs one or two fearless ones pecking through the mesh to cause a serious loss of fruit.

It is best always to provide a simple framework for netting, even over low-growing fruits. This can be done quite easily from thin-section timber treated with a copper-napthenate solution.

There are, of course, ready-made fruit cages which are a very good investment because they will last for many years. Usually these cages are constructed from tubular steel covered in green plastic, and consist of standards, which are the metal rods inserted vertically in the ground, supporting cross-pieces, the top rods that form the roof sections. Once these are in position, the netting is carefully arranged around the sides and over the top. These metal cages are surprisingly strong and rigid and will withstand quite rough weather, though of course there is very little wind resistance in this type of structure.

There are sizes for all needs. The lowest are about 2ft 6in and ideal for strawberry beds and most vegetables. The taller ones generally provide a headroom of 6ft. The smallest ones cover an area of 9ft; the very large ones an area of 96 × 48ft, and there are many in between. A good size for the smaller garden would be 15 × 8ft. It is an excellent idea to plan a fruit garden with these cages in mind, and mark out the fruit rows according to the sizes available.

CHAPTER 11

Protected Cultivation

Provide plants with shelter from cold winds and raise the temperature of the soil by this protection and it is remarkable how much earlier the crops can be harvested. Many can even be gathered out of season, or, at the least, several weeks earlier than the same thing grown outdoors. We are not here discussing greenhouses—they have a chapter to themselves later on—but simply the benefits that result from cultivation with the aid of cloches and frames.

CLOCHES: PLASTIC DESIGNS

Plastic cloches are much cheaper than glass, virtually unbreakable, light to carry about, and easy to stack or store away in the minimum of space. On the other hand some plastics are affected by sunlight and eventually discolour, crack or shatter; they do not retain warmth as well as glass though they do seem to warm up more quickly; and they scratch badly and in time become slightly opaque and do not then admit the maximum amount of light.

Because of their extreme lightness, anchorage into the ground is vital, otherwise they are easily disturbed or even blown away. I find that individual sections are not easy to butt together in the rows and quite often, after they have been in place some little time, gaps do occur; a certain amount of ventilation is essential admittedly but during very cold weather a better seal is required. Some of the tunnel cloches, on the other hand (these are made up of a continuous length of plastic and supported at frequent intervals by wire hoops) are not easy to handle, especially in windy weather and they do take much longer to get in position than the more conventional designs.

Of the plastic types I particularly like those made of the more rigid materials such as PVC. They are much tougher and a lot easier to handle than those constructed from thin sheet polythene—even, I would venture to say, than glass cloches. Their rigidity makes it possible to place them more accurately and to keep rows straight, and there is no risk of breakage when they are moved.

One type of cloche is made with wire-reinforced plastic and this is especially strong. An unusual feature here is the provision of numerous small holes in the roof sections, so that the plants are watered whenever it rains. One can, in fact, allow the hose or sprinkler to play over the tops successfully. Anchorage clips are provided with these cloches so that they can be fixed to the ground, and if the anchorage pins are removed on one side only in working along the rows the individual cloches can be pushed back like the bonnets of cars. These cloches can also be dismantled and stored flat, which means a considerable saving of space.

All plastic cloches should be kept as clean as possible and for this a good wash down with warm water and detergent should be adequate. Do *not* use any abrasive materials—these scratch the surface badly.

Sizes of plastic cloches vary but generally widths are 12–30in and lengths 18–24in.

GLASS CLOCHES

There are only a few designs in glass on the market, the most popular range consisting of two basic shapes known as the tent and the barn. The tent is a simple roof shape in two planes, and the barn a structure in four planes, rather like the end section of the walls and roof of a house.

The tent types are a little limited in use but are excellent for raising rows of seedlings or for the protection of single rows of crops at any early stage of their development. Generally a width of 15in is available with a height of 10in, in standard lengths of 2ft. The more versatile barn types are usually 2ft long and some 23in wide. Heights vary from about 12in to about 19in. Both types can be bought singly or in sets of twelve or more.

Assembly is much more complex than for plastic designs but once it has been mastered they can be erected or dismantled in a reasonable time. The metal fittings or framework are generally manufactured from heavily galvanised wire of high tension so that the completed cloche is a very stable structure.

BENEFITS OF CLOCHE PROTECTION

The barn design is the more useful of the two types of glass cloche because it has the greatest width and headroom. Quite a complex cropping system can be evolved for these larger cloches, plastic or glass, and one of the most intensive ways of using them is to intercrop. This means that more than one type of crop is grown at the same time under the cloches. For example, two outer rows of carrots can be grown with a centre row of lettuce or even beetroot, and if a quick–growing crop is used with a slower-growing one, the earlier crop can be harvested before the slower one needs more room to develop in later on.

Not only can an intensive intercropping system be used under the cloches, but adjacent strips of ground can be planted or sown so that, when one row of cloches has raised a crop either to maturity or to a stage when the protection is no longer necessary, it can be moved sideways—with little effort and risk of breakage—to cover a new crop nearby.

If these two systems of intercropping and adjacent growing are used, quite a modest area of ground can be made to give a large amount of produce—a tremendous advantage in the small gardens of today or where gardeners want to cut down on their vegetable gardens and the labour involved.

Cloches are ideal for bringing on green salad vegetables. The protection they afford ensures the very rapid growth which results for example in the crisp, tender lettuce leaves all gardeners aim for. Radish matures very quickly too and its flavour is considerably enhanced. And in cold districts—in the north of England for example—cloches are invaluable not only for bringing crops successfully through low winter temperatures but for sowing and planting generally. Quite often, ordinary outdoor sowings cannot be undertaken at the correct times in the north because of inclement weather, the soil being far too cold or wet to be prepared or for drills to be taken out. But if cloches are placed over the sites about two weeks before sowing time, the soil will not only be in a suitable condition for preparation, but it will be slightly warmer than the uncovered ground and will promote quicker and better germination. The same advantages apply to the planting out of seedlings or young plants.

Many gardeners extend the enjoyment of their gardens by exhibiting produce at local or national shows. Cloches can help enormously in enhancing the quality and size of the produce, eliminating the dangers of weather damage and improving accuracy of timing the crops for the show date.

SOIL PREPARATION

As successful cloche gardening is an intensive system, the soil preparation must be very thorough. Poor results can often be attributed to failure in this, particularly if not enough attention has been given to water supply.

Because the soil is covered, direct rainfall does not reach the plants, but moisture will penetrate sideways from outside the cloches provided the strips are prepared about 6in wider than the width of the cloche to be used. If, also, a high proportion of humus material is incorporated as the soil is prepared this will act as a sponge and absorb all available moisture. The humus can be applied in the form of peat, composted vegetable waste, hop manure or leaf mould. If rotted farmyard manure can be obtained, so much the better.

During long spells of dry weather a hose or sprinkler can be used over the cloche tops. The water will run off the roof, down the sides and into the soil on either side and then sideways into the prepared strip. If the gardener so desires he can run a trickle-irrigation line inside the cloches and along the top of the soil. The nipples on the line will keep the soil nicely soaked. Where larger plants are being grown, the line can be positioned carefully so that a nipple coincides with a plant, and the soil surrounding each plant will be kept moist.

FRAMES

I am sure I am right in saying that a lot of greenhouse owners begin with a frame and quickly fall for the fascinations of more and more glass when they realise its possibilities. The garden frame, limited though it is, can produce a surprising variety and quantity of produce and is an excellent shelter for many tender plants in the winter. When it is heated it becomes an even more useful piece of gardening equipment. It is also a useful accessory to a greenhouse, where plants raised in the greenhouse can be hardened off, ready for planting outside. Placed in the cooler conditions of a frame, they are gradually inured to natural conditions as the frame lights are opened bit by bit, until finally they are removed altogether.

There are several different types of frame on the market and each has its own particular qualities. The main differences are in the construction materials used, and whether the frame has solid sides or is entirely of glass.

Where the maximum amount of protection is important, in gardens that are cold or exposed, a frame with wooden or brick sides is the best choice. The more glass there is in a design the more heat loss can be expected. Then comes the problem of light, because an all-glass design is naturally going to provide more light than one which has its sides covered in. But the siting of the frame will do much to solve this problem. In a place away from shadows and overhanging trees, in a sheltered yet open place, the wooden or brick sides should present no hindrance to growth as far as the light factor is concerned. It is when the frame is put in a dull corner of the garden that culture becomes unsatisfactory.

Accessibility is another important feature to consider when a choice of frame is being made. Most models have lights on top which can be taken off completely or slid back along grooves or recesses. Others have lights so hinged that the tops can be adjusted to several positions.

STEEL, ALUMINIUM AND WOOD

These are the three materials used in the construction of frames. The steel designs are very strong and heavily galvanised to reduce rusting—unless this galvanising is of a high standard rusting will always be something of a maintenance problem. They are also quite heavy and the tops or lights may be a little difficult for the woman gardener to manage. Remember that the weight of glass has to be considered also.

Aluminium frames are light and require no maintenance whatsoever. They are attractively designed and, like the steel ones, have the minimum of cross section of material so that there is the least possible reduction of light. The tops are very easy to handle and are ideal for the woman gardener. Some steel and aluminium frames can be extended by connecting additional units as the situation demands.

Wooden frames are made either from deal or cedarwood. Of the two timbers, the latter is the best buy as it is rot resistant, but it does need the occasional treatment if its beautiful original colour is to be preserved. Deal frames need a good initial preservative treatment with a safe product such as copper napthenate, especially where the wood is in contact with the soil. Usually these wooden frames have boarded sides, which makes them quite warm. Usual sizes are 4 × 3ft and 6 × 4ft.

Brick-built frames are very permanent features and not so popular with the average gardener. This is understandable because they are quite expensive to build, and unless the gardener is a handyman the laying of the bricks is best left to a professional. This type of frame is usually built on to the side brick wall of a greenhouse so that plants can conveniently be transferred to the frame. Separate frame lights of wood can be purchased for placing on a wooden framework on top of the walls.

One advantage of the brick frame is that, suitably sited, the depth or headroom can be built up to suit individual requirements and with this extra height a useful range of pot plants can be grown, especially if the frame is heated by special air and soil-warming cables.

The home handyman can make his own wooden frames, preferably with detachable sides and ends so that the frame can be moved around if necessary or stored away for the winter. Usually a depth of 12–15in is adequate for the front wall of the frame, and 18–24in at the rear. Although, of course, these measurements can be adjusted as necessary, too great a depth should be avoided. Again, frame lights can be bought to lay on the top.

age 103
bove) An oscillating
prinkler which can be
gulated to give coverage
ver specified areas

ight) The pressurised
rayer takes the effort out
the job. This is a
udor design

Page 104
(*left*) The quickest way to make a fish pond is to use one of the pre-fabricated pool basins, such as this Highlands model

(*right*) The Sealion fountain-kit pump from Highlands ensures a sparkling display with minimum installation

A UNIQUE MODEL

There is one unique and attractively designed garden frame which must be mentioned. This the Access flat-roofed frame. It is in fact a glass 'box', constructed with such economy of framework that it gives the best light penetration of any frame I know. Naturally, the heat loss in winter is the greater, but even so it is an excellent design for spring, summer and autumn work and could be equally useful in winter with heating cables installed.

The manufacturers of the Access have had the sound sense to provide useful accessories, overhead watering among them, so that a complete growing system is offered. There are several sliding glass panels in the flat roof and vertical sides: as its name implies, there is complete access to crops in any part of the frame. The glass is held in simple metal channels and the frame can be dismantled and moved to other sites quite quickly.

Several sizes are available: some are 10ft long and 4ft wide with useful heights of 20 and 26in respectively. Smaller units are 4 × 4ft with heights of 20in, 26in and 46in. However, the number of Access frames on the market at the time of writing is limited.

PLASTIC FRAMES

These are usually panels of tough plastic sheeting in a wooden framework, or hinged metal-framed tops of PVC on a metal-sided structure. One very useful insulated frame has thick extended polystyrene sides which lock together. The frame lights rest on top and are double-glazed with glass. Very good frost protection is afforded. The whole unit can be taken to pieces very quickly, and extra units can be added to form a range of frames. Although these frame tops are heavy they would present no problems to the woman gardener. One has to be careful, in using these frames, not to catch the sides with the feet as the polystyrene is quite soft.

I prefer to work with glass frames as I find that a damp atmosphere quickly prevails under plastic in certain weather conditions. Nor do I think plastic frames suitable for the colder, northern gardens as heat losses are more rapid. Nevertheless, for late spring and summer use the plastic frame can give a very good account of itself and should certainly be considered for the warmer weather.

SITE PREPARATION

No matter how good the frame may be, results will be poor unless the site is carefully prepared. The most important requirement is good drainage, and especially where soils are heavy.

The area should first be dug out to a depth of about 1ft and the bottom broken up with a fork. Then work in some sharp sand of well weathered gritty cinders. On very heavy soils, place a 2in layer of ashes over this. Replace the soil and at the same time mix in more sharp sand until the soil is well speckled. Also add peat at the rate of one part to every three parts of soil. After the usual dressings of a balanced fertiliser, the soil will be ready.

If the frame is to be used as a standing ground for pots and boxes, it is a good idea to place a 3in layer of weathered ashes on the surface. This allows for maximum drainage and will discourage many slugs and snails.

Frames demand a lot of attention to watering and it is convenient to have a water connection as close to the frame as possible. Chapter 6 on artificial rain deals with the installation of do-it-yourself water pipes and the way in which take-off points can be established for hose or tap connections (page 71). One such point could be close by the frame to facilitate watering.

HEATING FOR FRAMES AND CLOCHES

The installation of a heating apparatus can transform frame or cloche into miniature greenhouses providing complete frost protection. Early sowings can then be made with even greater safety and the frames make very versatile propagating units. But, obviously, although heating can be applied to cloches in the form of soil-warming cables to ensure quicker and earlier growth it is used to best effect in the frame. A combination of soil and air-warming cables can be fixed inside the frame to provide a minimum air temperature of 7°C (45°F). With this it would be possible, for example, to commence propagation work in February and with careful planning, to keep the frame busy nearly all the year round.

To conserve heat it is a good idea to heap up peat or even straw around the outside walls of the frame. The glass should be covered at night with sacking or sheets of hessian, but all glass coverage *must* be removed as soon as possible next day, otherwise plants will become badly drawn.

Two types of heating can be installed: a low voltage kind which works off a suitable transformer reducing the voltage to a safe level, and mains voltage equipment which uses special protected or sheathed cables. The soil cables are laid in parallel lines, care being taken to see that they do not touch or cross each other, otherwise they will heat up at the contact points and probably burn through eventually. The air-heating cables must be kept a short distance away from the walls of the frame to prevent overheating and to ensure a good circulation of air behind them. Special clips are available for this purpose so that the cables can be pushed onto them.

CALCULATING HEATING REQUIREMENTS

The necessary loading or length of cable which will be required for a frame depends on several factors. The first is the type of frame, ie whether it has metal, wood, brick or all-glass sides. The second is the frame's size. The third is the desired temperature which is to be maintained inside the frame. The fourth and final factor is the 'temperature lift' desired. This is the difference between a postulated lowest outside temperature against which the desired inside temperature has to be maintained, and the desired inside temperature. The inside temperature to aim for is 7°C (45°F) and the outside coldest temperature should be decided at –6.7°C (20°F). The difference between these two temperatures is 13.7°C (25°F). This is the temperature lift.

To calculate the heating requirements for a frame 5 × 5ft (ie area 25sq ft) built with brick or 1in thick wooden sides (not less) we proceed as follows: a loading of 3 watts per sq ft is allowed for every 2.8°C (5°F) temperature rise desired; therefore multiply the area (25sq ft) by 3 and this sum by 5. This gives an answer of 375 and means that a 375 watt loading will be the minimum requirement. (These calculations are based on figures recommended by the Electricity Council.)

If frost protection only is required, a temperature rise of 11°C (20°F) inside the frame should be allowed for. A loading of 12 watts per sq ft of frame area will be adequate and for the frame previously mentioned a total wattage of 300 will be required. It will be appreciated that only a slight increase in wattage is required to provide a useful 7°C (45°F) in place of marginal frost protection.

It is advisable to use a thermostat for all types of heating. This not only provides complete automation but ensures the most economical running costs.

A word of comfort to the non-mathematical: specialist firms are only too willing to extend help and advice on all heating problems.

WARNING

It must be emphasised that all electrical work, ie connections etc, should be undertaken by a *qualified* local contractor or by the local electricity authority. Under no circumstances should the gardener attempt to do it himself. Electricity properly installed and with the correct fittings and accessories is a safe and reliable friend. Badly installed it can be a killer.

CHAPTER 12

Fighting the Foes

The gardener always has to be on his toes to protect his plants from the attentions of pests and diseases. Every season brings its own particular attacks and adverse weather conditions encourage the spread of various harmful fungi.

The wise gardener should never be caught unprepared, and successful control will depend not only on the use of the most appropriate sprays or dusts but also on the selection of an efficient applicator. No matter how good a fungicide or pesticide may be, its efficiency will be greatly reduced if it is not applied properly.

Several factors must be taken into consideration when spraying or dusting apparatus is being selected. The operation of spraying can be quite a tiring one if the equipment is not easy to use. The capacity to go for needs careful thought. Large quantities of liquid can be quite heavy to carry about. For very large gardens it will probably be better to buy a portable piece of equipment.

It could well be that one size of sprayer may not be adequate for all jobs. It is far easier to handle a small sprayer in the confined spaces of a greenhouse but the same sprayer would be a little tedious to use for outdoor work!

The woman gardener should be considered when spraying equipment is being purchased. Spraying can be quite a pleasant task if the right type of lightweight apparatus is selected, and many women would not mind being responsible for the spraying programme—an arrangement that would certainly reduce gardening duties for 'the man of the house'. I personally feel that women are much more thorough in many gardening operations and spraying is one of them.

MAIN TYPES OF SPRAYER

Sprayers come in many different shapes and sizes but there are basically only three types, syringe, trigger and pressurised.

The syringe works like a bicycle pump and is usually the cheapest to buy. There are two distinct types of action with this design: short burst action and continuous action. In the latter a constant spray or jet of water is emitted from the nozzle as the handle is operated to and fro. In the former type the water is emitted only when the handle is plunged downwards. This is rather tiresome and time-consuming to use. But it is very cheap and probably a good buy for a lean pocket or a small garden. The continuous-action designs are supplied with a length of thin-bore hose, usually about 8ft, one end of which, with its filter, is placed in the container of liquid. They are quite light, around 20oz, and not too tiring to operate for relatively short periods. All are provided with adjustable nozzles which regulate the water outlet from jet to spray.

The next type of sprayer has a trigger action similar to that of a pistol. Capacity is about $\frac{3}{4}$–1pt and the liquid is stored in the plastic body. These are very useful little sprayers for indoor work, either in the greenhouse or in the home for house plants. They can be used for the odd spraying of small attacks of pests or diseases but are rather tiring on the fingers after a little time. One or two designs have a plunger type of action and this is even more tiring to use! There is a small range of $\frac{1}{2}$ gallon trigger action types. A long flexible polythene tube connects the trigger end to the $\frac{1}{2}$ gallon tank, usually plastic.

This provides a much greater spraying capacity but is also, in my opinion, a rather tiring sprayer to use for long periods.

The most labour-saving designs are without doubt the pressurised sprayers. These are pumped up by hand until a good pressure is attained and then the spray is released at the touch of an off/on valve or trigger. The high pressure obtained by these models ensures that the insecticide or fungicide is forced well into the foliage of a plant, providing essential maximum coverage and penetrating many places which might otherwise be missed, particularly useful when tall plants or trees and shrubs have to be dealt with.

These pressurised sprayers are of large capacity, usually $\frac{1}{2}$–2 gallons; some of the larger models providing about 14 minutes of spraying at one priming. Useful features are the long lance, the easy-carrying handle and the shoulder strap. Considerable improvement in the design of the pump mechanism has been a feature in recent years and the use of plastic, nylon and polypropylene materials has resulted in sprayers which are not affected by strong or corrosive materials. This means that their maintenance is simplified and their working life considerably extended. Indeed, some of the more expensive models use a surprising number of different materials in their manufacture, many of them—such as nylon bearings—reducing the need for lubrication as well as ensuring smoother action and less wear and tear.

On many models extension lances, generally of about 2ft 6in, can be screwed on the existing lance to give even greater reach. Control of spray, a very important buying consideration, is extremely good in most makes. Turning the nozzle one way or another rapidly alters the type of liquid application. Very fine, forceful sprays are possible with many of the better quality designs.

There is no need to carry the larger pressure sprayers during spraying. They are provided with a special base so that they can be placed on the ground close by the work. Several types of pressure sprayer with capacities of around 4pt have a sling shoulder strap which is very useful where it is necessary to climb a ladder to get to a tree or shrub or where climbing plants are trained along a wall. They do not get in the way of the user and, once fully primed, will provide a continuous spray for 6–8 minutes. An optional extra in most cases is an extension lance. Where an exceptionally long spray duration is required at one priming (eg for extensive borders) the 14pt Kingsize Killaspray is useful. When fully primed it gives about 30 minutes of continuous spraying. This particular model is rested on the ground close to the work and would not be as convenient as a lighter sprayer for ladder work or manoeuvring between plants or rows of crops. It is available with a long-reach extension lance.

A very useful type of shoulder-strap sprayer is one which has a continuous action lance. A lightweight plastic-bodied version, the Solo No 90 Mini-Spray, holds a ½ gallon of liquid and should appeal to the woman gardener. The weight is about 1lb and the pump action is particularly smooth. Brass fittings to such important components as the pump and lances ensure good service. The adjustable nozzle provides a useful range of liquid applications from fine to coarse mist and ultimately a strong jet spray which is useful when attempting to reach tall trees and shrubs.

GAS-OPERATED SPRAYING

For the gardener who for one reason or another wishes to avoid the labour of pumping I would especially recommend a gas-operated pressure sprayer. A special canister of non-toxic gas capable of providing sufficient pressure to discharge the contents of a sprayer is fitted to it. Each can contains sufficient gas to deal with about 5 gallons of liquid. The adaption fits the Killaspray Super sprayer of 8pt capacity.

KNAPSACK MODELS

For comfort combined with large capacity the knapsack type of sprayer is hard to beat. The smallest size holds about 1 gallon and would interest the woman gardener who wants to carry out a more extensive spraying programme at one go. The use of polythene containers drastically reduce overall weight: the empty weight of the 4 gallon size is only 13¾lb, complete with operating equipment such as lance, hose, harness etc, which is very reasonable. Adjustable plastic or webbing straps ensure a comfortable fit and the double-action continuous-flow pump on the lance reduces fatigue considerably. As usual, the lances are extendable and adjustable nozzles ensure a wide range of spray applications.

The more one can reduce the effort required during spraying the better, and for this reason I must confess that my favourite type of sprayer is the knapsack which is provided with a priming system requiring the minimum of pumping. These designs have a conveniently placed handle or arm at the base of the tank. Only occasional strokes or pumps are required to maintain the required pressure and I find that I can work for long periods without becoming tired. Capacities of 1–4 gallons are available.

A good purchase in gardening equipment is one which provides the user with something as versatile as possible without being 'gimmicky'; it is often a basic piece of equipment transformed by useful accessories. There are several of these in the sprayer section. A very good example is the Polypak knapsack sprayer. This is available in capacities of 1, 2 and 3 gallons and the baby of these weighs only 7lb. The harness is detachable from the polythene container and separate containers can therefore be set aside for different chemicals. Only occasional pumping is necessary to maintain a very good pressure and the action is very easy.

Its greatest virtues, however, lie in its accessories. The most striking of these is the telescopic lance made from lightweight alloy and available in sizes of 9, 12 and 15ft. The sections lock by a twist of a special screw collar. A tap is conveniently situated at the base of the lance to control the flow of liquid. Another useful accessory is the lawn sprayer which consists of a spray bar or stem with six jets. Fitted to a special wheeled frame, the complete unit can be pushed over the lawn as it is primed by the knapsack sprayer carried on the back of the operator. Jets, on/off taps, hose–couplings, booms etc, are interchangeable, providing a most comprehensive spraying system.

ULTRA-LOW-VOLUME APPLICATION

One of the most remarkable innovations in spraying equipment has been precision low-volume application for pesticides. In very simple terms, it is a method of forcing a water-based chemical through a jet and placing a fan behind it to emit the solution as a moist cloud.

The very latest low-volume sprayer consists of a pre-packed oil-based chemical which is gravity fed at an exact and constant rate to a set of rotating discs. These rotate at approximately 7,000rpm and the liquid is atomised by the centrifugal force. About 5,000,000 droplets of liquid are produced from 1cc of pesticide every second! In this way a cloud of spray is deposited with maximum coverage. A considerable saving of materials is a very important advantage with this type of spraying.

Three quite different machines are available. The first is powered by a small petrol engine of about 1hp with an effective range of 12–15ft, and just under 10lb in weight. The second type is powered by electricity and is much lighter, at around 6lb; its range is 15–18ft.

The third design is a battery-operated model which weighs about 7lb; 12 volt batteries are employed and its effective range is somewhat less, at about 10–12ft. This machine is the handiest for the average gardener. It is interesting to note that droplet size is not affected as battery power is lost. What does happen is that the range of the spray is gradually shortened.

Up to now the range of suitable chemicals for this type of spraying equipment has been rather limited. It is to be hoped that these will keep pace with the advance of spraying equipment.

DUSTERS

These are not generally used by the average gardener—at least not in a mechanical form. No doubt the reason for this is that there are very few on the market. For most gardens they are not really worth while, especially as the equipment is quite expensive.

They are, however, a good investment if a lot of crops have to be dealt with because accurate distribution can be achieved at very economical rates. The Kyoritsu model, for instance, distributes ½lb of powder over about 500sq ft. This design is made of lightweight alloy and is operated by turning a handle geared at a ratio of 1: 24. A satisfactory coverage up to 8ft from the nozzle can be achieved. A larger capacity model holding 7lb of powder can be obtained for really large-scale work.

CHAPTER 13

Water as a Garden Feature

Nothing is quite so relaxing as a water feature in the garden. A placid pool in formal or informal surroundings, a sparkling fountain on the patio, a tumbling waterfall in the rock garden—all these delights are now well within the capabilities of the average gardener as a result of the revolution which has taken place in garden aids. Expertise and artistic flair are not necessary.

Water in the garden not only provides considerable enjoyment but a great deal of interest also, first in the actual construction of the water feature and then in the establishment and observation of plant and fish life.

PLANNING A POOL

Time spent on planning is far from wasted. The following basic points should not be overlooked. Keep as close to water and electricity supply as possible to reduce installation costs and minimise work. Give aquatics or water plants plenty of light if they are to flourish properly. They should receive full sun for the greater part of the day, or for not less than half of it. Avoid at all costs siting the pool under, or close to, trees or bushes. Falling leaves in the autumn pollute the water and affect the fish. See that adequate depth of water is provided for plant growth; a shallow pool would freeze solid in winter and become too hot in the summer. The minimum depth for a pool, no matter how small, should be 15in. For average pools a depth of 24in would be adequate and for large ones 30in should be provided.

Pools made from concrete or with plastic liners should have a very slight slope on the sides to prevent ice damage during expansion and contraction processes.

Various types of aquatic plants require different depths of water and as it is desirable to establish as wide a variety of plants as possible, provision for these different depths must be made. This can be done by constructing shelves along the sides. Prefabricated units have these shelves built into them. Marginals, plants that grow near the pool edge, require a water depth of about 9–10in and a shelf width of some 8–9in.

CONCRETE

The 'old-fashioned' way of making a pool was to use concrete, but this is very laborious work and repairs are nearly always necessary as the pool ages. The usual problem is cracking of the concrete and consequent loss of water, or else the concrete deteriorates and becomes porous. The surface can of course be mended with a thin layer of concrete, the application of a special sealing solution or the use of plastic sheets as liners. But how much easier and quicker it is to use good, modern, trouble-free materials.

PLASTIC

This is now the most popular material for pool construction. It is available in many sizes and in several qualities. The cheapest is a thin sheeting which is a little fragile and should only be considered where a short-term or temporary feature is required. It is certainly not a good long-term investment.

The thicker and tougher plastic sheets are suitable for permanent pools, and the laminated types which consist of terylene coated with PVC are very strong indeed. This particular type of sheeting has a considerable amount of elasticity which facilitates the construction of a pool, especially the informal type of pool with an irregular outline.

Sheeting can be joined or welded by most suppliers so that any area of pool can be calculated for. In some cases a tailor-made liner can be supplied for formal shapes with base and sides ready formed. All that is necessary is to drop the liner into the carefully excavated hole.

Many liners are available in various colours, usually blue, green and a natural or stone shade. There is even a coloured pebble finish! I have never understood why a manufacturer even thought of this idea. Who has ever seen pebbles go vertically up the side of a pool—which is the effect one would get if this patterned liner were used to line a pool completely! There is perhaps some point in using a small piece on the bottom of a pool or in a situation where a pebble effect can be seen in a shallow section of water. Even so, this is still a little artificial and it would be well worth the trouble of obtaining a few pebbles for the purpose.

The blue shade is very attractive, but here again I think an unnatural effect is produced by having a section of blue sheeting on view between the water line and the top edge of the pool. Stone or black would be much better here. The blue would look quite well in a terrace pool perhaps, where the intention was to provide colour and a touch of gaiety.

Sheeting is most suitable for formal pools if a neat, reasonably wrinkle-free finish is desired. It is, nevertheless, satisfactory for informal designs also, provided the outlines are kept as simple as possible. It will not be possible to avoid some folds or creases but most of these may be below the water level and will not be seen. Care is necessary, as the pool is filled, to keep the plastic sheeting smoothed out as much as possible. In many cases a few neatly executed folds and tucks overcome the problem of arranging the sheeting over irregular outlines.

Tough though much of the sheeting is, it is necessary to

remove all stones from the base and sides of the excavation before the sheeting is laid in position. A cushion of sand, finely sifted soil or even of peat should be placed in the bottom of the pool to a depth of about 1in. Some of this material can be stuffed along the bottom edges to form a slight curve thus avoiding any strain on the sheeting, or on the joints if a welded or tailor-made liner is being handled.

It is not possible to cushion the sides similarly but if the soil is inclined to be rough a covering of very cheap or scrap plastic sheeting can be used to protect the liner.

RUBBER SHEETING

There is a special man-made rubber sheeting known as Butyl. This is, without any doubt, the best and toughest of all the sheet materials available at present. It is extremely strong and has a life of at least 50 years! It is resistant to puncture (within reason) and heat, cold, erosion and sunlight have little or no effect on it.

It is very flexible, although a little heavy to handle where larger sheets are required. It is black, which gives a satisfactory natural-looking finish, especially for a stream or waterfall. It is versatile enough for most shapes of pool, although I do find it a little difficult to arrange in an informal pool which has *several* gentle curves because the thickness of the sheeting tends to make the folds and creases rather obvious. For formal outlines it is ideal, especially if a tailor-made welded liner is ordered. It fits like a glove!

It is also one of the few liners on which rocks can be rested with every confidence, and so is a good choice for stream or waterfall features. Admittedly when I have done this myself I have taken the additional precaution of placing an extra generous cushion of sand under the liner beforehand, and sometimes also an odd piece of Butyl immediately under each piece of rock.

Butyl is more expensive than plastic sheeting but a better long-term investment. And if you are set on having a colour other than black it is possible, apparently, to apply a special coating paint when the sheeting is in place. Only one *good* application should be necessary and it dries in about 24 hours. No harm will come to fish or plants if this paint is used.

CALCULATING THE LINER SIZE

Liners are allowed to overlap the edges of the excavation by about 10in. This facilitates their anchorage by soil, turf or edging stones. In the initial stages of construction, pieces of paving or brick are placed on these overlaps to hold the liner as it is filled with water.

There is a simple way in which the amount of material required can be ascertained. This applies to any shape or size of pool. The *length* of a liner is calculated by adding the overall length of the pool to twice its maximum depth. The *width* is calculated by adding the overall width to twice the maximum depth. In most cases there is no need to add extra inches for an overlap as the reasonable elasticity of the liners will create a surplus, but if desired an extra foot in width and length can be ordered.

Here is an example for a pool 10ft long, 6ft wide with a maximum depth of $1\frac{1}{2}$ft. Length of liner = 10ft + 3ft = 13ft. Width of liner = 6ft + 3ft = 9ft. As odd footage cannot be ordered a sheet 14ft × 10ft would be necessary. In this case it would be best to increase or decrease the original size of the pool to give dimensions of either 9 × 5ft or 11 × 7ft.

PRE-FORMED POOLS

These are rigid or semi-rigid pool basins or units made from thin polythene-type materials or from fibreglass. Formal and informal designs are available and most are made with shelves or basins to facilitate the planting of various types of aquatic plants. Those without marginal shelves are usually quite shallow. Some of them, known as trays, are especially designed for fountain installation. They can be used on a patio, for instance, to take the tumble from a wall-mounted fountain.

Small pool basins which are a little deeper are very useful as secondary pools in a rockery. Small aquatics can be planted in them and quite an attractive water garden established. There are circular units which permit the gardener to design out-of-the-ordinary layouts.

Many of the informal designs have most attractive shapes and curves. Some are more than 10ft long with a width in some places of 5ft or more. In this sort of size the gardener can establish a wonderful range of aquatic plants and fish.

All these pre-formed pools are very easy to install but the excavated soil must be carefully backfilled under the unit so that no large areas are unsupported. It is as well to firm the soil in place with a long piece of wood. Their edges can be concealed in a similar way as those of the liner pools. In informal layouts, outcrops of rock can be placed here and there along the edges to provide a most natural effect.

PLANTING

The best way to plant the various aquatics is to use planting crates. These are usually made from plastic and are available in various sizes, usually in the region of 8in, 10in and 12in square.

Plants for the garden pool can be conveniently divided into seven categories as follows: water lilies or nymphaeas, deep marginal plants, marginal plants, submerged oxygenating plants, floating plants, marsh plants and waterside plants. The marsh and waterside plants are *not* established in the pool itself but are arranged outside around its edges where they add to the charm and natural appearance of the water feature.

The planting crates are filled with soil (no manure!) then planted and placed either on the bottom of the pool or on the shelves, according to the depth of water they require. If necessary, some of the crates can be put on bricks to adjust the depth more accurately. A handful of gravel scattered on the surface of each crate when it has been planted, will prevent soil erosion or disturbance by the water or the fish.

FOUNTAINS

No one, I think, would be without a fountain once they have seen the dancing, sparkling water effects it can produce. And you don't have to be a plumber to install one. You simply buy and fit together the necessary equipment.

Two types of pump can be used—the first a submerged model which is placed directly in the water, the second an external or surface pump which is set up outside the pool. Both types are powered by electricity.

The submerged models are the easiest to install because the minimum of piping is required. Some models are connected to a transformer which reduces the mains voltage to a safe level of about 24 volts. These pumps have an outlet on which the fountain unit is fitted and are usually rested on bricks so that the top of the fountain comes above water level. The electric cable is carefully concealed by arranging it between rocks on the edge of the informal pool or by taking it under the grass or paved edge. For complete safety, where mains voltage cable is used, it should be taken in alkathene piping to prevent damage and as much of the cable as possible should be buried below ground. It will be necessary to connect more cable to that which is already fitted to the pumps. This must be done with a good quality *waterproof* connector. Where a transformer is used with a pump, the electrical connections *can* be undertaken by the gardener. For mains-only types, a competent electrician *must* be called in.

All pumps utilise the water from the pool itself and re-circulate it over and over again.

The submersible pumps can then be connected to an ornamental fountain by a suitable length of piping. There are several very attractive stone ornaments available which can enhance a water garden.

The pump, especially a submersible model, should be selected according to the size of pool. The larger the pump the greater the fountain display and the greater the intake of water to the pumps. One of the smallest pumps is the Otter which is ideal for pools up to 70sq ft in surface area. For larger displays the Little Giant model should be considered and for larger features still try the Sealion and the Big John.

Gardeners will come across the term 'head' used in connection with the performance of a pump. It refers to the vertical distance between the pool water surface and the pump's outlet, against which the pump is working, and which, in addition to loss of pressure in pipework and fittings, affects the output of water. If the Otter pump, for example, has its outlet point (the end of the pipe which carries the water out of the pump to a fountain or to the top of a waterfall) set at 3ft above the pool's water level, the output of water will be about 330 gal per hr. If the outlet is placed at the higher level of, say, 7ft then the output drops dramatically to about 120gal per hr.

The more powerful pumps are capable of delivering a much greater volume per hour but even they are affected by a rise in the head. Take the Big John pump—if this is working with a head of 3ft the gallons per hour work out at approximately 3,000. Raise the head to 7ft and this figure drops to around 2,100. It is interesting also to compare the Otter and the Big John working at the same head. The difference in capacity is most marked and one can see why more powerful pumps are necessary for larger water features. The larger pumps produce the most spectacular fountain effects, but there must also be a pool of large surface area to catch or contain the wide spread of falling droplets.

The choice of a fountain can make all the difference to the display. The fountain tops already supplied for the smaller pumps like the Otter give a very pretty throw of water but where complex patterns are required it will be necessary to purchase separate fountains or jets. Quite complicated patterns are available. Some, for example, have a central cone of water with multiple sprays working at the sides. Several fountains have as many as four jets incorporated which throw a delightful and intriguing pattern of water high into the air.

These fountains can be fitted to standard ½in standpipe or they can be attached to any fountain ornament. Selecting a fountain is a fascinating business. One of the best ways of going about it is either to obtain a catalogue from a specialist firm (eg Highlands Water Gardens of Rickmansworth) where drawings of the patterns are provided, or to visit the firm's display centre or one of the several garden centres where these fountains are in operation.

Fountain ornaments

Fountain display is considerably enhanced if a fountain ornament is used. The best—and it is wise to purchase only the best for the sake of appearance and weathering qualities— are made from artificial stone, usually in a weathered Portland stone finish or a lead finish.

There are birds, seals, ornamental bowls and dishes, little boys, astute dolphins, mermaids, water carriers, and wall fixtures in the form of lions' heads and other ornamental plaques or masks. These wall fixtures are useful for patio work where they can be mounted in a solid or screen-block wall. The water is allowed to fall into a stone basin at paving level and from there drained to a large sump at the rear where the pump is placed, and re-used. But many of the other types of ornamental fountain can also be incorporated in a patio or terrace feature.

Where a fountain is used in a pool planted with aquatics, the water lilies should be situated where the fountain water does not fall. Many aquatics, especially water lilies, do not like disturbed water.

WATERFALLS, CASCADES AND STREAMS

One of the most exciting uses of water in the garden is for waterfalls, streams and cascades—quite dramatic in sound and sight, and most refreshing during very hot weather.

Waterfalls

First the course of the stream and the pool at the bottom have to be constructed. This can be accomplished in two ways—either with plastic or rubber sheeting, or with special pre-formed units of fibreglass.

For the face of the fall use actual rock or simulated rock pieces such as the Literoc products, which I defy anyone to distinguish from the real thing. There are no fibreglass units for waterfall faces as far as I am aware. Alternatively the fall can be made from a sheet of the plastic or rubber material which has been used to line the excavation. Black Butyl is ideal. A few rocks placed here and there, especially on the lip of the fall, will break up the flow of water and produce a more realistic effect.

The top of the fall should be as high as possible to produce the dramatic rush and tumble of water associated with the natural feature. The pool itself should be relatively small. It is all a matter of sensible proportion. In a restricted site it is possible to have simply a face or rock over which the water tumbles to a tiny pool below filled with small pieces of rock and stones.

The water from the pool is drained to a deep sump at the

back of the feature where a submersible pump takes it up to the top of the fall again. It is unwise to use the very small pumps for this type of feature as they do not provide a sufficient quantity of water.

Cascades

These are a series of 'steps' or tumbles for the water along a stream course and can be made from liners laid over an excavated run in which a suitable number of steps have been cut to form the cascades. The edges of the liner can be concealed by soil or rocks and waterside plants.

As in the case of the waterfall, care must be taken to see that a basin or hollow run is provided so as to prevent the water seeping over the edges. One of the simplest ways of making a cascade feature is by the use of pre-formed fibreglass units. These are finished in the natural rock face and can be arranged in series, each overlapping the unit below, to form a long and complex layout if necessary. A slight fall or slope must be provided so that there is a suitable flow of water along the stream's run. The units must also be levelled carefully across their width to prevent overspill. Cascade pools can be bought in colours of blue, sea-green or natural stone. They are quite effective when well arranged and concealed carefully at the edges.

Streams

These are similar in construction to cascades but without the series of falls. They can be used as a single run or flow of water or installed in series to link up small pools or cascade units. In this way a most intriguing layout can be achieved, especially if the units are arranged in irregular lines to meander between the rocks in a rockery. With a little careful planning, a mixture of pool basin, stream course, waterfall and cascade units can be built up into a complex water system which will provide many hours of interest and pleasure.

Streams can be made quite easily with liners covering an excavated course. This should not be too irregular otherwise a great deal of folding and crossing of material will be necessary to negotiate the twists and turns. The edge of the liner can be trapped and concealed under the soil or grass.

Note

In all water feature layouts it is necessary to control carefully the flow of water from the pump, but this is facilitated by the use of a valve fixed in the pipework or supplied on the pump itself. Lighting, which can play an important part in water features, is discussed in detail in Chapter 18.

CHAPTER 14

Plant Containers

The colour displays in the garden can be increased by the use of plant containers, and colour and fragrance can be brought nearer to the house. Indeed, it can be said that containers bring the garden into the home and the fascinating world of gardening to those who have no garden. They can be filled with exactly the right soil and placed in the right positions for the plants you want to grow, and with them you can combine the convenience of concrete with the pleasure of having plants.

By careful selection, the appearance of the containers can considerably enhance the display of the contents, especially in the home.

It is very difficult to advise on the actual choice and a writer should probably not attempt to do so. What would appeal to one person would not necessarily do so to another. A container should also blend well with its surroundings and no two gardens or homes are alike. Manufacturers have tried to meet the very wide range of possible requirements and have produced containers in great variety—one can safely say that there is something for everyone and for practically every situation.

SIZE

The type of plant or plants which are to be grown in the container, and also the space available for the container, will be the two main factors governing size. Specimen plants such as conifers, roses etc, need plenty of root room, smaller bedding plants, bulbs and many colourful annuals can do with less. It is better to purchase a container which is slightly too large than one which will restrict the roots; a healthy plant is one which has a vigorous and free-running root system.

Flat dwellers will want window boxes to fit sills or to stand on balconies. People with small paved backyards will turn their attentions to containers of fitting proportions. One or two large containers generally look better than a multitude of small ones in yard, patio or terrace.

PLASTIC AND FIBREGLASS CONTAINERS

The many different finishes available range from mirror-smooth plastics to rugged contoured natural stones. All have their individual fascinations and appropriate settings. The smooth container, for example, looks rather out of place in an old-world type of garden where the weathered appearance of many of the natural and reconstituted stones is ideal.

But plastic and fibreglass these days can simulate almost any material. One of the latest ideas is wood-grain reproduction for tubs which is difficult to distinguish from the real thing. Fibreglass is used to create wonderful reproductions of antique originals with a wealth of delicate and intricate pattern and in quite complex shapes, as, for instance, Grecian urns with handles.

The great advantage of plastic and fibreglass containers, especially for the woman gardener, lies in their light weight and easy handling. They are also weatherproof, completely frostproof, and of great strength, fibreglass particularly. They are easily cleaned and the impervious surface is even dirt-resistant, which is a useful point when they are required for town work.

WOODEN CONTAINERS

A very attractive range is available in wood, which blends so well in any garden scheme. Cedar and teak are particularly good buys because they are very durable and completely weatherproof. Teak is a hard timber which can be treated occasionally with a special oil to preserve its colour; cedar has an especially attractive warm reddish-brown hue, and this wood also requires treatment every second year or so to maintain the original colour. One of the leading manufacturers of teak containers is Lister. Oak casks, when they can be found, also make splendid plant containers. Another very hard, durable timber which will give many years of good service is iroko, made up quite often into tubs with black galvanised hoops. The Branson range of containers is in this African wood.

If softwood containers are purchased, it will be necessary to examine them carefully each year to make quite sure there is no sign of decay. Annual treatment with suitable paint on the outside will keep them in good order, and a copper napthenate initial treatment (the horticultural grade of Cuprinol is ideal) for the interior after it has been cleaned and dried out, will prevent rot. It is as well to treat all joints especially liberally because this is where the rot starts.

Outside window boxes are traditionally made from timber although there are a few plastic designs available. It is essential to see that they are fixed securely, and if they are used above neighbours' flats a drip tray must be provided to catch excess water.

CONCRETE

Concrete plant containers have recently been greatly improved. Not only have thicknesses been reduced without detriment to strength but there is increased variety and quality in design, pattern and shape.

Low cone-shaped bowls are especially elegant and can be obtained in several sizes. You can buy fluted Grecian urns moulded in concrete, with surprisingly good reproduction of detail. And there are attractive square and oblong containers that make useful edgings to patios and paved areas.

The only slight drawbacks to this type of plant container are that it is quite heavy even when empty, and of course can be chipped or broken easily unless carefully handled. Concrete containers are usually placed if not in a permanent position then at least in one where they are likely to remain for some time.

Surprisingly enough, few concrete models are affected by frost but a certain amount of flaking may occur if very cheap and poorly finished types are purchased. A great deal of care is exercised in the formulation and cement mixing for the better class models and some form of sealing is used also.

There is a certain solidarity about concrete containers which makes them very popular nowadays and they seem to improve with age, quickly mellowing from their first white brightness. They have a place in the modern formal garden and also in the most informal layout. They are perfect partners for paving or walling features, and the more ornamental kinds are particularly effective near informal water features.

ASBESTOS-CEMENT

This may seem a rather unusual combination of materials for garden containers but it results in a completely weather- and frost-resistant product. The finish has a natural texture and soon weathers to an 'aged' appearance. The Urastone company makes a great range of shapes, from the complex to the very simple; from egg-timer outlines to saucer-shaped bowls. There are window boxes with scalloped or wavy sides and dainty shell-shaped receptacles for indoor plants.

These containers are relatively fragile because they have a remarkably thin section, but sensible handling will ensure trouble-free use. They are, again, surprisingly heavy but the thing to do is to put the container in position first and then fill it with soil and plant it.

I did experience a little problem with a green algae growth on the sides of asbestos-cement containers, especially after prolonged wet or damp weather, but I found that this could be removed quite readily.

A CONTINENTAL FLAVOUR

A number of suppliers are now importing a new range of garden containers. Some of the very attractive designs are Spanish in flavour—antique reproductions in reconstituted stone with an instant built-in aged appearance, and very difficult to distinguish from the genuine article!

Flower troughs, vases, small and large tubs are examples of the types of container available in this range. They are quite substantial creations. For instance, a small tub about 14½in high and 19in in diameter weighs about 82lb! A beautiful container in the form of a trough 5ft long, 19in deep and 11in wide weighs as much as 54lbs!

Do not be deterred by the weights of these products. They are well worth investigating and I have found that they can be placed in position surprisingly easily if several people can lend a hand and if smooth planks are used as a skid. A round length of timber used like a roller would probably be the best method.

Christian's and Patio Design specialise in the supply of this intriguing equipment. The latter firm also make a speciality of Spanish-style pots, vases, urns and jars more suited to indoor use or sheltered positions.

INDOOR CONTAINERS

Appearance is even more important here and fortunately the manufacturers have provided us with a very interesting range. One popular way of displaying plants is to arrange them in a jardinière. The firm of Hago have made a special study of this type of container and have produced some extremely attractive ones. Basically they are formed from steel scroll work, with a waterproof trough or liner made of plastic. The finish of the scroll work is either white enamel or brass plate and the troughs are available in tropical green or French mustard. Some are table models, others free-standing types. One of these free-standing jardinières is supported on a simple pedestal some 26in high. The pedestal can be unscrewed and feet fitted to convert it to table use.

Glass carboys make unusual containers and grow indoor plants to perfection. Although they are getting more difficult to obtain because plastic containers are now used for the carrying of commercial liquids, a few can still be purchased from time to time. Very large bottles can be used for similar plantings. Collections of suitable house plants can be planted in well moistened compost in the bottoms of the bottles; they are then corked and a moist growing atmosphere is maintained for many weeks. The all-glass surround enables the householder to enjoy the plants from any angle, and in fact a miniature greenhouse is established indoors.

One of the main problems with indoor plants is keeping them well supplied with water. There are ingenious self-watering containers which neatly solve this problem. They are marketed as the Riviera system (by Camplex and Inter-Market Distributors) and comprise a range of troughs and pots with supports and bases in black metal to convert them into free-standing containers or for attachment to walls or balconies. Made of high grade polystyrene, they have a water reservoir at the base and a nylon fabric watering device which maintains the soil in a moist condition. The plants draw moisture from the soil as they require it. A water level indicator is provided in the side so that a quick check can be made at any time. Colours are black, red, ivory, and there are pewter, copper and waterproof velvet finishes also—the velvet comes in dark grey, dark green and dark brown.

There is a lot to be said for the automation of water supply. Not only does it reduce time and labour but it does so much to ensure the successful progress of the plants and, by so doing, encourages the gardener to even more ambitious efforts! The considerable increase in the use of central heating and double glazing has added to the difficulties of house plant cultivation but this automatic method of supplying water and, incidentally, maintaining a valuable moist atmosphere around the plants, overcomes the problems of dry atmosphere and rapid water consumption.

One of the latest additions to the Riviera range is the terrace trough. A series of these can be used outdoors, placed in line on a slope or on steps and connected by tubes which go up into the container but remain below the ventilation pipe overflow incorporated in each trough. When the water has reached its proper level in the first trough, it runs into the connecting tube of the next container and so on. The water can be supplied automatically via a ball valve tank connected to the mains water supply or they can be watered at one go from a pipe attached to the tap. The terrace trough is attractively styled and has a length of just under 3ft. The colour is white.

I would strongly recommend this system to those of you who have no garden as such but perhaps a paved area at the front or rear of the house. The troughs can also be used on a balcony or even as a roof garden. Provided there is a reasonable amount of sunlight and shelter from cold winds, planting schemes would be very successful.

This Riviera system is the answer to the holiday watering

problem, especially for house plants. A further development in this direction will be the cabinet providing a fully controlled growing environment for indoor plants in respect of heat, water and light. One firm, House and Garden Automation, is doing a lot of work in this field and I don't doubt that they will shortly be in a position to put on the market, for the amateur at home, an attractive display and growing cabinet which will be both a container and a piece of furniture in its own right.

HANGING BASKETS

A very attractive way of displaying plants is by the use of hanging baskets. These are usually either wire bowls or plastic bowls with drainage holes provided. One unusual design has a built in saucer or undertray in which water can be poured to act as a reservoir for the plants. As the undertray also prevents drips this type of basket can be used indoors as well as out.

One of the latest models is a pendant type of container made from plastic material. It has a central galvanised telescopic centre support which avoids the old clutter of chains. This design has a tray at the base, and is in a stone green, carefully selected to blend with most colour schemes.

THE ART OF DISPLAY

No matter how attractive the container is, the overall effect can be disappointing if the selection and arrangement of the flowers is poor.

For window box display a few central or feature plants should be planted. *Grevillea robusta* with its attractive feathery green foliage is a good subject, or ivy-leaved pelargoniums or half-standard fuchsias. For the main mass display, petunias, tuberous begonias and *Campanula isophyllas* could be used.

ge 137
ight) Plant containers
e this asbestos-cement
sign by Urastone enable
e gardener to bring colour
many parts of the
rden

(*below*) Iroko, a West African hardwood, is used in the manufacture of this set of furniture by Lister

Page 138
(*left*) Decorative screen walling combined with textured coloured brickw will enhance the garden layout—a Marshall desig

(*below*) A modern summerhouse in the Hall range

For spring displays plant the many types of outdoor bulbs such as tulips, hyacinths etc. If a permanent display is required, ericas (heathers) can be planted round two or three dwarf pyramidal conifers, such as *Juniperus communis*, as centre pieces.

For bowls or containers the basic planting principle is to have the tallest plants towards the centre and the smallest around the perimeter. Centre plants can be fuchsias, pelargoniums, schizanthus, *Senecio cineraria* and marguerites. For smaller bushy plants, select from bedding dahlias, nemesias, salvias, asters, celosias and calceolarias. Trailing plants have an important part to play in container planting, especially if hanging baskets or tall containers such as urns are used. For this type of trailing edge planting use trailing lobelia, cascade petunias, pendulous begonias, fuchsias and *Phlox drummondii*.

CHAPTER 15

Leisure in the Garden

In these days of stress and noise it is so nice to find a place of refuge in one's own garden. What could be more pleasant than a comfortable chair, a warm summer's day and the sight and smell of beautiful flowers? Yes, garden furniture has a very important role to play in providing the relaxation so many of us need.

There is a tremendous range in design, material, pattern size and cost. Look for comfort first; price will have a restricting influence no doubt, but it is false economy to go for the cheapest. The higher the price the better the finish, the more luxurious the cushioning, and the sounder the springing. There are a few designs in the cheaper ranges which are quite good value for money, but on the whole you have to pay more if you want years of wear and good service.

Eye-appeal is almost equally important, and there is much to be said for gaily coloured garden furniture on the patio or terrace or by the swimming pool, where an 'atmosphere' is to be created.

COMFORTABLE FURNITURE

Wooden furniture is, on the whole, much less comfortable than other types. Having said this, I would hasten to add that a few designs are surprisingly restful when one considers that there is no spring or cushion effect in wood. The comfort is built in, in the form of contoured seats and backs. A slight curving of those parts which support the body makes all the difference. But usually wooden furniture is intended for meals in the garden and most ranges are built on table and chair sets. It is a splendid idea to have these on the paved or terraced sections in a garden; the furniture is always at hand and one can decide at short notice to take a meal outside without the bother of collecting the various items from the shed or summerhouse and setting them up in an appropriate spot.

Some designs combine a wooden framework with canvas seats and backrests, or incorporate comfortable cushions. This makes quite attractive furniture especially when the wood is painted with a white gloss paint and the canvas or cushioning is gaily coloured or patterned.

A little more comfort is supplied in metal folding chairs with canvas or plastic coverings. Some of them have foam padded seats and backs.

But for complete comfort there is no doubt, in my mind at least, that lounger chairs and adjustable beds are the things to buy. The user can regulate their angle, to suit his body contours and his mood, at a number of positions ranging from the upright to the horizontal.

Garden furniture de luxe is undoubtedly the swing hammock, or couch hammock as it is often called. This, of course, is the most expensive but can be a jolly good investment, especially for the elderly.

The deck chair should not be forgotten. It has the virtues of restful angle, adjustability and easy folding, but that front bar is very uncomfortable for the back of the leg!

DESIGNS IN WOOD

Several types of timber are used in the construction of garden furniture: ordinary soft wood finished in an attractive high gloss paint, usually white; teak, which is an extremely hard, durable wood requiring no special preservative measures, and one or two African hardwoods such as iroko.

One of the largest suppliers of teak furniture is Listers who provide a complete range of designs from bench seats which can seat several people to table and chair sets or suites. Some of their designs are available as do-it-yourself kits which are most fascinating and easy to assemble. I have had a bench seat made up from one of their kits for many years in my garden. The family use it quite often and it is as good today as it was when I first acquired it.

Low garden tables are also available in kit form and these are very useful where low reclining or lounger seats are used —just the right height for magazines and cool drinks. They can be stored conveniently in the winter as the legs are detachable.

One of the cleverest ideas I have come across for some time is a 'nesting' set of table and four chairs. The chairs have been built with their back rests at a complete right angle so that they can be pushed under the table at its four corners where they fit snugly and form a complete box. These chairs are quite comfortable and the back of each seat has been contoured at the right angle to fit the back of the user. The table is about 36in square, and some have, or can be supplied with, a central hole in which a large garden umbrella can be inserted. Sets of three nesting tables which fit one inside the other are useful when there is a large group of people for a meal in the garden and also because they take up so little room. The variation in their sizes makes it easier to arrange them on terrace or patio. Several types of round table, high or low, are also available.

I am very pleased to find that garden tea trolleys are available—handsome in teak and invaluable for the hostess who does a lot of entertaining in the garden. Some trolleys have removable trays; some have folding sections which, when opened out, provide a large carrying surface or table-like top. Complete matching sets of table, chairs and trolleys can be purchased.

The Wrinch range of garden furniture includes not only these trolleys and matching sets, but also a good looking range of white painted furniture in similar sets of table and chairs as well as canvas-covered, folding chairs, some of them with sun canopy and extension leg rest attachment. The painted furniture just mentioned should not really be left outdoors in the winter. In fact some manufacturers specifically recommend that it be taken inside.

Wooden furniture which dismantles easily is worth investigating. The Branson range is of this kind, the very simple joints being held together by knock-out wedges. The timber used is the extremely hard, durable West African iroko. The design is old-world with attractive priory benches and cottage-type suites.

Treating wooden furniture

There seems to be a lot of confusion concerning the treatment of wooden furniture. Teak and iroko wood is completely weather resistant but will lose its attractive colouring unless given an annual application of teak oil. Before this is done, it should be scrubbed down with soapy water, rinsed and allowed to dry. If there is any roughness of the surface after this treatment a rubbing down with sandpaper will bring up the surface again. Soft wood such as deal must be painted occasionally with a quality gloss paint. Wash down with soapy water each year also.

DESIGNS IN CAST METAL

There was a distinction and elegance in the old cast iron designs of the Victorian period. Their greatest disadvantage was their considerable weight. It is pleasant to see them back again in a range of reproduction designs cast in aluminium, and combining elegance with lightness and durability. The current and increasing interest in Victoriana means that this type of garden furniture is quite the 'in' thing, and likely to stay so for a long time. The metal on these reproductions is finished with a weather-resisting white enamel, and the seats are of natural or painted wooden slats. The wrap-round or curved backs to the chairs add considerably to their comfort, although in many cases the seat sections could be contoured a little more.

One of the leading manufacturers of these aluminium reproductions, A. E. (Metals), have designed a most elegant range appropriately called Ferndowne because of the beautiful fern motif used. This firm obviously appreciates the need for more than Victorian comfort and provides sets of shaped foam rubber cushions for chairs and benches. The tables in this range are available with either metal tops in delicate tracery, natural wooden tops, or marbled formica.

Another rather similar range of metal furniture is called Fantasia and is made by A. Bavystock. Seats and backs are formed of very delicate and intricate cut-out designs and all the metal is nylon coated to make it completely maintenance-free. There are matching tables available. Elegant legs and marble or glass-covered scroll-work table tops add to the eye appeal of these designs. This type of furniture is just what is needed on the terraced area by the swimming pool, as water splash, particularly from chlorinated water, will not affect it. It is easy to move about and fits perfectly in a paved and walled setting.

METAL FRAMES

The largest selection of garden furniture is in this category. Basically chair designs consist of a tubular metal or aluminium alloy framework over which the seat and back are formed from canvas or plastic materials. Considerable adjustment is provided by a device located just under each arm, which can be operated while sitting in the chair.

The simplest of these models is the ordinary chair in low- or high-back design. Whilst no two people would agree on what is a comfortable chair, I myself feel that the low-back designs do not provide the same comfort or support as the high-back models. It is surprising what a difference those extra few inches make!

Most of the chairs have arm rests, though these are not always as comfortable as they might be, usually because they are just those few inches too high or too low for the person using the chair—which goes to show how desirable it is to try out a chair before purchase. This is where the garden centre is going to be so valuable. Most stock quite a good range of garden furniture, and if you can get along to try it out I would strongly advise the effort!

The most comprehensive sitting adjustment is provided in the lounger or bed-type design. These usually have three sections—a back rest, a sitting or seat section and a leg or foot section. The two extremities are adjustable from a vertical to a fully horizontal position, and the foot or leg section can be taken through the horizontal to rest on the ground, so providing very comfortable support for the legs. A special fitting enables the user to adjust the angle very quickly simply by moving the section to and fro to unlock the setting. A similar action when the new position is arrived at locks the section securely in place. The operation can be done whilst on the lounger but it is probably more comfortable to do it standing up.

Quality ranges from the simple canvas-covered model to the more expensive foam-filled or tubular plastic webbing designs which are extremely comfortable. The Elegant range includes a fascinating air-filled plastic woven tubular type, which forms a comforting cushion around the body's contours. The plastic does tend to stick to the skin when the weather is hot and when shorts or bathing trunks are worn, but this can be overcome by using covers or cushions.

Some of the more expensive divan or lounger types have deeply quilted foam covers, no-sag springing and even an inflatable pillow! A great deal of attention is paid to appearance and some are very gaily patterned and fringed, with matching canopies available.

These leisure beds fold away neatly and occupy quite a small storage area. The aluminium alloy designs are much lighter to carry about than the tubular metal types, and if the larger items of garden furniture have to be carried any distance before they can be set up this is rather an important consideration in buying.

Comfort depends not only on adequate cushioning and adjustment, but on sufficient room. A wide chair makes all the difference, especially for a wide person, and there are one or two extra-wide designs available from some manufacturers. The Elegant people cater for this with their king-size divans and leisure beds.

CANE FURNITURE

I am very attracted to cane furniture, not only because it is such a 'natural' looking product, but because of the delightful shapes made possible by the material. It is also surprisingly strong and quite light to handle. Ratten cane is used by Whines & Edgeler, one of the leading importers of this furniture.

Many different types of seating are available, from the simplest of chairs to most elegant of settees. The natural spring of the material promotes comfort and gay back cushions and seat cushions add to it. I particularly commend the curved back rests of several of the designs.

A favourite with my family is the Lobster Pot pouffe, made from willow and very strong indeed. Their large model measures 24in across and 16in high. It is made by the same firm.

Funchal cane furniture also comes in all shapes. For extremely lazy gardeners there is a very nice rocking chair, ideally contoured in flowing lines to rest the body and ensure complete relaxation. It is about 5ft long front to back and this enables him to really put his feet up! There is also a delightful swing chair with a springy backrest. The extending chair is another relaxing design, with provision for those aching feet! A suite of furniture comprising table, a two-seater settee and two single chairs is a very good idea for the terrace or patio garden.

Although most of this furniture can be used outdoors, it is wise to bring it inside in the winter. All units mentioned are ideal for the conservatory or the home extension.

SWING HAMMOCKS

The acme of luxury and comfort is the swing hammock or garden lounge. The roof or canopy provides pleasant adjustable shade from hot sunshine and a great deal of protection from cool winds. The gay coverings and tassels add to the relaxing atmosphere. The back rests are usually adjustable and, if necessary, the swinging seat can be locked. There are several designs in the cheapest range and although these are reasonable value for money, I think that to invest in a more expensive model is a far better proposition. They are even more comfortable and will last and look good for a much longer period.

The only drawback to this type of garden furniture is that storage is a problem. They are quickly affected by damp, although most of the coverings used are waterproofed, and in winter ought to be stored in a dry place. They do dismantle into smaller sections but the seat and back rest parts still take up quite a bit of room in that airy dry garden shed.

During summer nights the lounge can be covered with a special night cover which will do much to reduce damp and dew deposits. Even so it is necessary to remove this cover as early as possible in the morning to allow the air and sun to dry the covers out.

Comfortable though it is, this type of garden furniture can be a nuisance at times. The smaller and more portable furniture designs are more labour- and time-saving overall. This, of course, is only a personal opinion, but there is no doubt in my mind that the swing lounger is more suited to the larger garden and to the larger pocket! There is also another important point to consider before buying one and that is that the garden must be reasonably level; uneven ground places an undue strain on parts of the framework and it will, in any case, be a little uncomfortable to sit on if the seat slopes. The seat section will not swing satisfactorily either. However, it is a simple matter to make a small paved area for this type of design.

TRENDSETTERS

The rapid development of new materials will undoubtedly influence garden furniture designers and some quite revolutionary designs can be expected to make their appearance.

Self-supporting hammocks are already available. This is a very sensible idea. How often does one find two conveniently situated trees?

Glass fibre, in my opinion, still has a very important part to play in bringing down the cost of garden furniture. If this can be done all we shall then need, in Britain at any rate, is better summers!

CHAPTER 16

Summerhouses and Home Extensions

Considering the vagaries of the English summer, we might well ask if summerhouses are really worth while. My answer would be a very definite yes, because they enable the gardener to make much more of his garden during the summer months.

A summerhouse provides shade from hot sun and, if well ventilated, a cool retreat during periods of warm weather. Should the summer be inclement, with coolish winds, the summerhouse gives protection. Where else is there a more convenient place to keep the fold-away garden furniture? Where else can you take meals in comfort or find solitude and quietness for writing or reading? The summerhouse makes a perfect changing room for those who have a swimming pool, and it makes a splendid place for the children to play in too!

SELECTION AND SITING PROBLEMS

As much care is needed in the selection of a summerhouse as in the selection of a greenhouse. There are so many variations in design to be considered, and in relation to garden layout. The old-fashioned or extremely informal garden is just the setting for some of the rustic designs. The trendy and sophisticated models which seem to be appearing in greater numbers need a formal background.

Sizes are not a great problem. In the small garden perhaps

the summerhouse could take the place of the garden shed, provided of course that the minimum of tools are kept, otherwise there would be very little room left for the occupier!

Most designs are attractive enough to be sited quite close to the house and incorporated perhaps in the terrace or patio area with attractive paving providing a sitting-out space round it. This arrangement avoids wear and tear on the lawn.

A south-facing site is ideal but could be too hot for some people. Wooden structures heat up quite a lot and unless plenty of ventilation is provided can become uncomfortably warm inside. Those who like plenty of shade and coolness could place the summerhouse near trees which would break up the sun's rays and maintain a cooler atmosphere. The structure and its surrounds would get covered with the autumn fall of leaves but you can't have everything!

It is wise too, to site the summerhouse so that prevailing winds do not blow into the open doors or windows. Take particular note of conditions in various parts of the garden: exposure to wind; areas that are particularly sunny or shady; the duration of shade or sunshine, and so on. The result of such a survey will indicate the most suitable place for siting and the best way of placing the structure.

The usefulness of a summerhouse can be extended if lighting is installed. There is no reason why a suitable heater could not be fitted to enable the gardener to enjoy the house in the cooler evenings—if an accurate rod-type thermostat is fitted the heater could be set to provide sufficient warmth to reduce dampness or condensation in the winter months.

TYPES OF SUMMERHOUSE

Present day summerhouse designs are quite exciting, and I am particularly pleased to see that several manufacturers are at long last providing the gardening public with first-class modern styles.

But the rustic designs available are particularly appealing. Who can resist their pretty roof shingles or cedarwood tiles—or the lead-lighting on the windows and doors—or the curved roof supports?

Then there is the middle range, where designs are not quite so rustic, and yet not extremely modern. They probably have a pent roof, and large opening doors with several small panels of glass in them instead of the leaded lights. There are no embellishments, but well-finished tongue and grooved boarded sides or overlap wooden cladding. A few of them can be rotated by means of a special base. You can, in fact, follow the sun by turning the summerhouse. The special gear provided for this purpose makes it surprisingly easy to move even the larger types. The firm of Pratten have made a speciality of this system.

The ultra-modern designs incorporate several interesting features. Some, for example, have flat roofs. Overhangs are usual, and although some of the other models previously referred to have these they seem to make more impact when used in modern styling. Large picture windows admit much more light and enable the user to enjoy views of the garden, and a little more attention is paid to ventilation.

A popular innovation is the verandah of wood along the front of the summerhouse. But it is above all the use of coloured panels that transforms the summerhouse, creating a feeling of gaiety and lifting it immediately into the pool and terrace class.

MATERIALS

The timber used in summerhouse construction can be an ordinary softwood such as deal, which needs painting or priming with a special wood preservative, or an attractive cedarwood which requires the occasional application of a preservative to maintain its beautiful original colour. If this is not done, the wood will weather to a grey colour which is, in my opinion, a little disappointing. The would-be purchaser of a summerhouse *must* be prepared to spend some time on the maintenance of the structure, especially if it is to be sited near the house.

A wooden floor is essential for comfort, though floors are generally sold separately. It provides a dry warm footing and is much cosier than a cold concrete base. As the floors are usually made from ordinary untreated deal it is very important that they should be liberally treated with a preservative such as the horticultural grade of copper napthenate (Cuprinol), paying special attention to the joists and the underparts of the flooring. I would not advise the use of creosote because its powerful smell lasts such a long time and becomes very noticeable in hot weather. The copper napthenate will smell for a little time but this quickly disperses.

The preparation of the base for the floor needs care. This floor, like the shed floor, will have to take a great deal of walking about and pressures and weights of varying kinds, so a firm foundation is essential. Individual bricks or large blocks can be used to support the floor bearers or joints, but a more easily constructed and more stable base is made if thick baulks of treated timber or several concrete fencing posts are laid down instead, spaced to support the floor bearers. These bear the weight more easily and levelling operations are simplified also because less *area* levelling will be required.

A paved path leading from the house to the summerhouse will do much to keep the floor clean.

AN ALTERNATIVE TO THE SUMMERHOUSE

If you don't wish to go down your garden to find a place to sit in then why not a home extension? It can be used as a colourful conservatory as well as a pleasant place to relax in, and is convenient for water and electrical connections as well as general maintenance. Garden furniture can be kept there and is always ready for use. In fact, not only does the extension provide the house owner with extra living space, as the manufacturers say, but it provides him with more garden and plant space, and greater opportunity to widen his interest in plants and their cultivation.

HOW TO SELECT YOUR HOME EXTENSION

There is virtually no siting problem which the modern home extension cannot overcome. Most manufacturers make their designs in a remarkable range of units, multiples of which can be joined together to fit any site. The various catalogues contain all the data required, and indeed there are *so* many permutations that it can become a little confusing and I strongly urge you to take your time over reaching a decision.

Buy as large an extension as the pocket will allow. The smaller types may have to do where the site available is very restricted, but by the time a few pieces of furniture are in place and a few plants, there is no space to stretch one's legs.

There is a lot to be said for having the maximum amount of light inside an extension, for the plants' sake especially. A clear roof made from PVC sheeting is suitable, and for the maximum growing facilities the clearest grade should be selected. The less transparent the sheeting the less successful the growing. Unfortunately there is one difficulty with PVC sheeting—condensation. Condensation forms on glass roofs as well as on plastic ones, but in the case of the latter it forms as large droplets and unless the roof has a good slope or pitch, these fall in a shower and can be quite a problem in very cold weather. I can speak from experience on this point!

There seems to be little one can do. Second ceilings have been designed but those I have tried have only been partially successful. In any case, they do cut down the light quite a lot, though with the very large picture windows which most home extensions have this perhaps does not matter very much except in winter and early spring. A solid roof reduces condensation but supplementary lighting will then be required if a wide range of pot plants is to be cultivated in the short days. Growing cases suitably lit provide an excellent way of growing plants in difficult conditions, and are in themselves very attractive pieces of furniture.

Cedarwood is the best choice for home extensions and very handsome buildings it makes! Don't forget that large picture windows demand a good ventilation system. The large glass area heats up very quickly and conditions can get uncomfortable in hot weather unless a good circulation of air is maintained. There has been considerable improvement in the design of ventilators in recent years.

I would always select a home extension which has double doors. These greatly facilitate the taking out and bringing in of furniture etc for the garden. Large door areas are also most useful as an extra form of ventilation, and if the home extension is sited on the garden side of the house an even better view of the garden will be afforded.

One range of extensions have substantial side walls of concrete with several interesting finishes. These provide better insulation and with the very attractive inner wall liners available they can be transformed into quite luxurious rooms.

Flooring important

Few people pay sufficient attention to the type of floor they are going to have in their extension. If you are a keen gardener you must have a floor which will not be affected by watering and yet still look attractive. I have found that solid concrete with a suitable damp course and covered by flooring tiles is very satisfactory. The tiles are colourful and decorative but easy to wipe over and not damaged by watering or overhead spraying.

Page 155

(*right*) This Hall greenhouse has low side walls of cedar and generous headroom

(*below*) An attractive frame in glass and metal. This design is from Crittall

Page 156
(*left*) Do-it-yourself assembly from an Eden k with sliding door and many other good feature:

(*right*) Spring-loaded sun-blinds and automatic ventilator opening are valuable in temperature control on hot summer days

(*below*) Humex version of the electric propagator for the smaller greenhouse

PLANT DISPLAYS

The arrangement of plants in a home extension is quite different from that required in greenhouse work. Display is important and plant holders or supports should be decorative. There should be no problem here because there is a wonderful range of containers available (see pages 134–6) as well as plant pot covers which quickly transform a plain clay or plastic pot into something eye-catching. Special racks can be fastened to the sides of the extension on which pots can be arranged. Trailing plants look well on these.

As space is always precious in a home extension I would not recommend the use of staging but there are some delightful plant tubs and plant stands which are easily moved about to make room for people using the extension or to allow the plants to receive the maximum amount of light.

PLANNING PERMISSION

I should emphasise that not only must planning permission be sought from the local authority but that their regulations in respect of insulation and fire risk must be complied with. Fortunately most of the leading manufacturers do comply with the regulations and supply, as part of their very efficient service, the fully detailed specification and site plans which have to accompany any application for planning permission.

CHAPTER 17

Swimming Pools

Until quite recently, the garden swimming pool was the prerogative of the extremely wealthy. The breakthrough in the design of the above-ground pool has changed the picture completely. Not only has there been a dramatic lowering of prices but their complete simplicity means that even the small garden can accommodate a modest version.

You may argue that the use of an outdoor swimming pool in England is rather restricted by the weather. Obviously, the warmer the weather, the more pleasant the water is, but a surprising amount of swimming and enjoyment can be got out of the garden pool in the average English summer.

SITING AND LANDSCAPING FOR THE POOL

The pool must be situated where it will receive the maximum amount of sunlight for the most part of the day. A position under or close to trees and shrubs should be avoided at all costs, otherwise in the autumn the pool will be full of fallen leaves. And not only leaves! I have a very useful cherry tree near my own small swimming pool and I am afraid I shall have to remove it—not because of falling leaves but because the birds drop so many cherries into the water when they are frantically trying to beat us to it at harvesting time!

The pool should be as private as possible; a position concealed from neighbours and their friends is not a bad idea.

Shelter from prevailing winds is of paramount importance. And obviously the site should be near to a source of water for filling, a drain or sump for emptying, and handy to an electrical supply for the filtration unit. Choose as level a site as possible to keep spadework to a minimum.

The landscaping of the pool surrounds solves many of these problems. I think the ideal solution is to integrate the pool with a terrace or patio feature. I have done this myself now, having tried to cope with wet and sticky surrounds from the splash and spray from the pool. A paved area around the pool or even just around the 'busy' area near the steps is a great help and enhances the setting. It also provides a convenient area for sitting out on.

I decided to pave part way round my own swimming pool, and then thought that the feature could well be a little more ambitious, so a part-solid and part-screen wall was constructed on two sides of the pool area. This L-shaped feature gave us the shelter we required from the prevailing wind and also privacy. There was an additional unexpected bonus and that was the remarkable heat reflection received from the walling. I am sure this has a lot to do with the higher water temperatures we experience. Of course, winds quickly cool the pool water and if these can be prevented from blowing across the water surface by walling or by any other form of screening, the temperatures should be a lot more stable.

Although most manufacturers say that the plastic liners of their pools can be left in position during the winter, I prefer to remove mine, and after cleaning and drying it carefully, store it away in the house. Severe weather is bound to cause some deterioration in the material. I don't leave my pool filled during the winter either. It seems a waste of money to keep the water purified if you can't use the pool—and how many of us would attempt winter swimming in an outdoor unheated pool! Even with the larger above-ground pools I think that the liner should be removed after the water has been emptied

ABOVE OR BELOW GROUND?

The cheapest and easiest to install are the above-ground types. These basically consist of an outer metal case or ring inside which a tailor-made plastic or PVC liner is fitted. The base of these pools is the ground on which the casing rests, but to prevent damage a cushion of sand is placed below the base, to a depth of about 1in.

The metal casing is available in a wide range of finishes, qualities and complexity of construction. A few have flat rims which form useful sun-decks for sunbathing. Some of the more expensive designs have sophisticated sun-decks surrounded by railings and reached by steps. It certainly adds to the atmosphere of the pool!

Sizes range from the modest 12ft diameter types to 25ft or more. One firm, Cranleigh Pools, have produced an oval pool which is 27ft long and 15ft wide. This is a very sensible idea because it provides much more room for the swimmers—children and non-swimmers could perhaps be kept to the 'ends'! Pool depths are from about 2ft 6in to 4ft. The larger the pool, the deeper the water, generally speaking.

The choice of pool size will obviously depend on the price which can be afforded and the available room. From my own experience I would strongly recommend you to buy the largest pool you can manage. My 12ft pool gives us a great deal of pleasure and we would not be without it, but it is too small for any serious swimming and is overcrowded when four people are in it, though as a place to cool off and relax in on one's own it is ideal. The depth of side is only 3ft and the depth of water rather less as one can only fill up to within 6–8in from the top. A depth of 4ft is much better.

For children only I would suggest the special pools which some of the pool firms offer. These are virtually paddling pools with shallower and safer depths. They are very quickly erected and filled, and store away in a very small area.

The below-ground pool

It is possible to construct your own below-ground pool from special kits or packs which firms like Capital Pools offer. These are amazingly complete deals and quite within the capabilities of any sensible and reasonably practical person.

They usually take the form of a large welded tailor-made plastic liner which is placed in the excavated site. It is necessary to construct simple yet strong retaining side walls inside the excavation and on to these the liner is fastened. Concrete walling blocks are usually recommended and the narrow gap between the walls and the sides of the excavation is then carefully back-filled with some of the excavated soil to add strength. As with the above-ground pools, the base is lined with a little sand to act as a cushion.

Complete filtration equipment and fittings are supplied in the pack and these are built into the pool as the work proceeds. The only problem with this type of pool is that of excavating the site. Local contractors can often hire excavators which will do the work quite quickly, but you will still have to dig out and clean out the corners and this can be some job! And before you rush off to hire an excavator just work out how you are going to get it into the garden. On a new site it might be easy, but what if you have an already established garden? It's quite a thought, isn't it! These kits, however, are very good value for money and the completed pool is practically as good as a commercial one except of course that it does not have that beautiful tiled interior!

The do-it-yourself below-ground pool needs to be finished off by a paved surround and, of course, those attractive pool-edge pieces. These extras can be quite expensive, but even so the total cost should be very much under that of a professionally made pool. Some of the cheapest complete kits cost only a few hundred pounds.

The best type of pool as far as finish and appearance is

concerned is, without doubt, the professionally constructed one. Several specialist firms (eg Rutherfords, Purley, Gilliam) undertake the entire work of putting an architect-designed pool in your garden, landscaping and all, in a surprisingly short time. The work is very costly but is probably a good investment and will certainly increase the value of the property. It is usually better to have as large a pool as possible if this sort of money is to be spent. Cost varies greatly according to type, size and shape, and labour costs are increasing all the time, so it is difficult to be helpful about this, but very approximately a pool with all equipment and about 15 × 10ft would cost £1,000.

One advantage of having a pool constructed professionally is that you can have an unusual shape, beyond the ability of the average amateur to construct. And the tiled or other sophisticated finish to the pool interior provided by the professional pool builder is also beyond the capabilities of the amateur. These pools are extremely strong and with sensible maintenance will last for years. Filtration units are concealed and heating equipment can be installed during construction to extend the use of the pool. Many specialist firms supply glazed pool covers which are virtually large greenhouses but much more attractive. These can be either permanent covers or in the very expensive models, movable ones which run on rails.

KEEPING THE WATER CLEAN

The water in the pool would quickly become unhygienic unless special chemicals were used to cleanse it. Fortunately this is a very simple operation and completely foolproof, provided the instructions are carefully carried out.

Two chemicals are used—chlorine to purify the water and algitrol to prevent the formation of algae. The former is available as a powder or special pellets and the latter is a liquid. The chlorine has to be applied nearly every day and a simple testing outfit must be used to check requirements. The anti-algae preparation need only be applied once a week. Improvements are constantly being made, however, and one of the latest is a large pellet which dissolves very slowly and releases chlorine into the water at the required rate.

A good deal of dirt and debris falls into the water. This is a much greater problem with the below-ground pools because the dirt is blown in from the surrounds. But even the above-ground designs can get very dirty; I never realised before just how many thousands of tiny flies there are about in the summer, to fall into the water and build up unpleasantly.

The hard way to clean the water is to use a simple suction brush connected to the garden hose. A small bag is attached to it and when submerged the vacuum brush (very similar to the vacuum cleaner head of the cylinder models) sucks up the debris which has sunk to the bottom. The floating debris can also be sucked off with this apparatus or removed with a very fine net which can be purchased for the purpose. There is no need to empty the pool water during the summer if all these tasks are carried out *regularly*.

Although this is the cheapest way of maintaining a pool in good order I do not recommend it from early personal experience! It is in the first place very time-consuming; the brush/vacuum head is only about 8in wide and this has to be moved *very* slowly up and down the bottom of the pool. In the second place it is only suitable for the smaller pools. We used to spend at least an hour every other day at this job all through the summer!

The answer is to buy a filtration plant which automatically skims the surface of the water and keeps it crystal clear. The water in fact becomes quite sparkling as it goes through what is virtually a 'polishing' process: it is sucked out of the pool continually, passed through a special filter or cartridge which may consist of charcoal or, in the newest models, diatomaceous earth, and finally returned to the pool via a second pipe or outlet.

Filtration units are sold by capacities related to the amount of water in the pool. These range from about 1,500gal per hr for the smaller pools to about 4,000gal per hr for the very large pools. Firms such as Blue Line, Cranleigh and Capital, to mention but a few, can supply all the necessary units.

Some extra equipment will be required, such as a pool vacuum which is connected, when required, to the inlet pipe of the pump by a length of flexible pipe. With this accessory the dirt which has escaped the surface skimmer of the filtration plant can be quickly sucked up. Although the skimmer removes an amazing amount of surface dust, oil and dirt, some heavy particles may fall into the water, sink immediately to the bottom and escape the skimmer's action. The skimmer is sometimes an extra which *must* be purchased. I cannot understand why some firms do this. A filtration unit should be available as a *complete* package deal. It is so irritating to find that one has to pay extra for all the little bits and pieces. In some cases the steps into the above-ground pools are extras.

In the 4ft deep Cranleigh above-ground pools the skimmer unit is built into the sides of the pool wall. This very neat arrangement keeps the swimming area clear of all obstacles; refinements such as depth control and flow controls are set in easily accessible positions. This type of neat installation is usually found only in the much more expensive below-ground pools.

The Cranleigh pools and a few others have very strong side walls which lock together quite quickly. Top and bottom rails ensure extra stability and the vertical supports also provide great strength. These are very important buying points to consider because the pool's wall has to withstand a lot of stress and strain, especially if the swimmers are a little boisterous!

WATER HEATING

An unheated pool obviously has limited usefulness. At 15°C (60°F) the water is quite cold. My pool is pleasant (and refreshing) to swim in when the temperature is about 20°c (68°F) and quite warm at about 24°C (75°F). We have been pleasantly surprised to find how much swimming we can get in during the year. Usually we can start about late June and go on until mid-September.

A pool cover is a useful extra. It keeps out a lot of dirt and, above all, prevents a good deal of heat loss, especially during the night. Several different types and qualities are available. All float on the surface, and some of the covers for underground pools can be rolled over like a giant sunblind.

But to obtain maximum use of a pool the water has to be heated, and this is a very expensive proposition, in runnisg costs as well as installation. Several pool specialists supply suitable equipment for all sizes of pool. One firm, Gazelle, produce a useful booklet on pools with information on current heating costs. Their heating plants are made to give a lift of about 14°C (25°F) to pool water from a temperature of 10°C (50°F) at the rate of .4°C (.75°F) per hour. Very approximate running costs are indicated, based on an estimated 1,000 gallons of water per 180 day swimming season. For oil, £3.50, for gas £4.50, and for electricity £5.50, the latter being for off-peak electricity supplies. All cost figures depend on local charges of course.

The cost of the heaters themselves runs into several hundred pounds and to this must be added installation and equipment charges for pipework, cables etc. But who can put a price on pleasure and leisure? You may consider several hundred pounds well invested in a feature such as a swimming pool, and then be prepared to reduce heating costs by further investment in a permanent or mobile pool cover, which would certainly also provide a place for entertainment for most of the year—despite the weather! Carefully landscaped around, it could be a very pleasing part of the garden.

REGULATIONS

Surprisingly enough, there are very few regulations concerning swimming pools in the garden. The water board should be contacted about the amount of water which has to be used. In many cases no extra charge is made for small pools but for the large capacity ones a meter may be required. Planning permission is not usually necessary but here again I always feel that it is wise to contact the local council office to make quite sure there are no unexpected bye-laws.

It is essential that water be drained away properly and not cause damage or embarassment to neighbours. The question of what type of special drain to use is a matter for the local authority to decide or advise on.

CHAPTER 18

Garden Lighting

Garden lighting has quite recently caught the imagination of gardeners. Its increasing popularity is probably due to the fact that much of the latest equipment is specially designed for complete safety. This has been achieved by the use of low-voltage transformers which reduce the mains voltage to a safe 12 or 24 volts.

WHY LIGHT A GARDEN?

There are several very good reasons for seriously thinking about garden lighting, although I must agree that the idea will not appeal to everyone.

There is much to be said for using it in the interests of safety. Steps and slopes can be tricky and perhaps a little dangerous to negotiate in the dark and a suitably positioned light will illuminate the area well. Long paths or drives can be brightened with lamps placed at intervals, and a garden light near the greenhouse or shed enables the gardener to work a little later on in the winter evenings.

Garden lighting has a very important role in extending the enjoyment of the garden. The terrace or patio or summer-house can be illuminated for barbecue parties on summer evenings, and much more fun can be got from the swimming pool if it is lit up, perhaps with coloured lights, for late evening and night bathing.

LIGHTING EQUIPMENT

The most versatile garden lighting equipment to date consists of a set of lamps attractively moulded in tough plastic materials and supplied with small ground spikes and wall fixing brackets so that they can be quickly arranged in any setting, from a low-ground position to a high one. A transformer is supplied, which has to be housed in a dry place, such as a shed or extension. One outlet of the transformer is connected by cable and earthed plug to the mains electricity supply and the other connects with the cable to the lamps. The actual connection of the lamps to the cable is carried out by the usual insertion of wire ends into a suitable socket in the lamp housing. The Moon Glow lighting units use a very clever and simple method of connection. A cover is unscrewed at the back of the lamp and the special cable pressed on to two metal prongs inside. When the cover is screwed down it forces the cable on to these pins and these make electrical contact with the wires inside the plastic covering of the cable. The cable itself is green and easy to conceal among plants in the borders. It could of course be buried shallowly in the soil and its run marked with small pegs to avoid damage during cultivation.

This type of lighting equipment is suitable for both large and small gardens, but of particular value in the smaller garden because it does not look obtrusive, in fact, far from that, it adds style to any garden settings. Coloured lenses can be clipped in place to provide exciting colour schemes.

There are several other forms of garden lighting, among them a range of very modern lamps shaped rather like mushrooms with large caps. These can be fixed on tall stands, or to the wall by means of attractive brackets. This type of lighting, however, is not transformed to lower voltages and installation should be carried out by qualified electricians. One of the problems I encountered with these lights was the difficulty of inserting their stands in the ground without damaging the cables. A waterproof junction box fixed to the stem at a convenient place would be both safer and easier. This would increase the price undoubtedly but would be worth it.

Reproduction lamps, especially the steel lamp designs are most intriguing and worthy of a place in the garden, though there are some rather crude designs in plastics which I find rather irritating and would not care to recommend. The old fashioned gas lamp reproductions can look quite charming in a suitable setting. An ideal site for one of these would be in the drive; they could also be set on terrace or patio, though I myself prefer the wrought iron lantern here, fixed to the wall by iron brackets and conveniently out of the way of people using the terrace.

Specifications for these mounted lamps should be studied with some care and the quality of the finish noted. Denloy Products is one of the specialist firms that supply quality lamps—beware of the poor quality design which rusts badly after the first season.

When several lamps of this kind are to be mounted on a terrace wall the job is not quite straightforward. There are problems over electrical wire connections or links, and suitable junction boxes must be used. A single lamp is not quite such a problem if its cable can be run in one continuous length to the mains supply. Even so the cable must be protected from weather and possible mechanical damage and must never be buried haphazardly in the ground. Special cable should be used and the best type is the mineral insulated and protected Pyrotenex which is very expensive but well worth the outlay. And again it should be emphasised that all lighting installations which are not transformed to safe low voltage *must be installed by a qualified electrician.*

Lighting in home extensions can do much to increase the pleasure of using them. Wall-mounted lamps will probably be best here because the roof or ceiling is usually quite low and a mounting in the roof could be inconvenient and perhaps a little dangerous.

LIGHTING AND WATER

This section is not to warn gardeners that water and electricity do *not* mix! The point should be noted carefully though. At least the two should not be used together unless a very safe system is installed and this is where the low-voltage transformer comes into its own.

There are several kits specially designed for water-lighting. One system, the Proops, uses spheres which contain light bulbs. These can be allowed to float on the surface of the water or can be submerged to any desired depth by attaching them to a similar sphere filled with ballast. They are rather fun to have in the swimming pool when it is not in use. A few of these with coloured lenses attached create a wonderful atmosphere around the patio and are ideal for party occasions. Used on a fish pool, they bring the water and the pool surrounds to life. The spheres can also be attached to ground spikes and used anywhere in the garden.

The Aqua Glow kits consist of a lamp in a plastic-type housing which can be allowed to float on top of the water or, by carefully trapping the cable at the bottom of the pool, pulled down to any desired submerged depth. This firm (Elsworthy Electronics) also produces a Glo Jet or fountain ring in which one of the Aqua Glow lights fits. The fountain ring is connected to a submerged electric pump and a wonderful effect is produced as the fountain jets play through the beam of light. If a coloured lens is used the effect can be quite startling.

DON'T ANNOY THE NEIGHBOURS!

If used with care, garden lighting need not cause annoyance to the neighbours but do try to avoid that carelessly placed light whose beam strays beyond your boundaries. A friendly courteous talk with neighbours is the best way to avoid any misunderstandings when novel features such as lighting are considered, especially if some of the lighting is to be situated close to the party fence or hedge.

There is a safety factor to be borne in mind when lighting is used in front gardens situated on a busy road. These lights are not powerful but if angled badly they could dazzle a motorist, so it is wise to take a little care over siting them.

Most of the lighting units which can be fixed to low ground spikes have a low spread of light. The Moon Glow units with their sealed beams give an illumination of 1,500 candle power with a spread of 50° horizontal and 25° vertical. This means that a bush or tree can be illuminated without too much of the surrounding garden being lit up. This highlighting of special subjects is one of the most dramatic ways in which garden lighting can be used.

Low wattage bulbs are generally sufficient for the other types of lighting, especially on the patio where a subtle subdued light will create much more atmosphere than a bright one.

BARBECUES

Barbecues and garden lighting go together. In America and Canada barbecues have been the rage for several years, and on the continent they are part of everyday living. Most of the models available in England are imported, and most are extremely light and dismantle very neatly. They consist basically of a metal fire basin supported by legs, and the number and types of the various bits and pieces which go with these basic parts will depend on how much you are willing to pay.

A wind shield is essential; so is a spit for roasting joints and chickens etc. Whether this is turned by hand or by a very convenient small battery-powered motor will again depend on the price you want to pay. Some of the more sophisticated designs have grills which can be regulated for height. A grill-like side shelf is a very handy accessory especially if a lot of cooking has to be undertaken.

Most housewives will probably be content with ordinary domestic cooking utensils, but it is possible to purchase special barbecue tools. Some of these are very desirable, especially those with long handles to keep the hands away from the very fierce heat of the charcoal; the special skewers obtainable for kebabs really add the finishing touches to the cooking and a pair of barbecue tongs facilitates the handling of food on or from the barbecue itself. Some of the more sophisticated barbecue designs have a tray or shelf below the fire basin on which the various cooking utensils can be kept.

Nearly all barbecues are heated by charcoal, which is purchased in small bags from the barbecue manufacturers, horticultural sundries shop or garden centres. The secret of cooking success is, apparently, to get the charcoal red hot before any cooking is contemplated. It always amazes me just how long the charcoal retains its heat.

Useful accessories for the barbecue occasion include a light, two-wheeled barbecue trolley, fully collapsible when not required, and convenient for taking glasses, bottles and all the usual bits and pieces, plates, knives, forks etc to the site. One or two designs have cut-out sections to accommodate glasses and bottles securely.

Although the English summer is somewhat of a joke, there are enough warm days and evenings to justify a serious approach to pleasure and leisure equipment such as swimming pools, lighting and the barbecue.

CHAPTER 19

The Use of Stone

Many people have the impression that stone is a very impersonal, colourless, cold material. They are wrong. New developments in manufacture have produced a fantastic range of textures, colours and shapes. Modern paving and walling can bring nearly as much colour to a garden as flowers.

The tremendous improvement in manufacturers' catalogues enables the gardener to select his stone with greater confidence if he has to do it this way. Most catalogues are illustrated in full colour and many photographs of completed paving and walling are given. But where it is at all possible a variety of stone should be seen before buying. This is the only way, really, of being sure about the texture. The address of the nearest agent can be obtained if a request is made to any of the manufacturers.

CHOOSING AND BUYING

Pattern, colour, size and texture all need to be considered in relation to the feature.

For a gay patio there are lovely shades of paving and attractive patterns of walling to choose from. A quiet mellow atmosphere is created by the use of a honey-coloured stone and rough textures. A wall can be lightened and brightened with occasional panels of open-work screen walling incorporated in the structure. The same type of block will also provide a wind barrier which at the same time permits light and sunshine to reach the area protected.

Paving and walling are costly materials, especially where high quality is required, so the initial heavy outlay must be regarded as a sound investment in the health of the family and the value of the property. Quality is particularly important if stone is expected to retain its colour. The cheaper stone does, as I know from experience, lose its colour fairly quickly, and disappointment follows. Several years ago I foolishly ordered some quite cheap paving simply because I wanted to make a feature very quickly and this was the only stone available locally at the time. Within a year, the colours had faded badly and after eighteen months it was impossible to say what they had been originally. A slight word of warning here about rough textured paving. Although this is most attractive I find it best to use it well away from the areas of regular garden traffic because it tends to pick up and hold dirt. For patios and other sitting-out areas, it is ideal.

It is quite a good idea to select paving from a firm that can offer a large number of different sizes. This frees you from the chore of having to cut slabs to fit. Despite what some manufacturers would like us to believe, cutting slabs is not an easy task for the amateur and I doubt whether there are many who can cut a stone really cleanly. In any case a great deal of valuable time can be taken up in stone trimming, not to mention the wastage of stone.

There is a lot to be said for mixing paving if really attractive and unusual effects are desired. Octagonal and rectangular paving can be laid on patios and if at least three different sizes of rectangular slabs are used, a pretty mosaic can be produced. A square-end stone is available with octagonal paving so that it can be linked with square or rectangular paving. Do not be deterred at the thought of laying mixed sizes. The work will be slower, of course, but provided you have levelled and squared off the site accurately there are no problems. Care and patience are the best tools!

PAVING

The most popular paving slab has a slightly rough face or textured surface and is available in a natural or stone colour and in shades of pink, green, red, grey, blue, purple etc. The mixing of colours needs a little care but colour photographs of successful blending are often found in the firm's catalogues.

Typical sizes of slabs (in inches) are as follows: 12 × 12, 12 × 6, 18 × 18, 18 × 12, 24 × 24, 36 × 12, 18 × 9, 9 × 9, 27 × 18, 27 × 9—variety enough to fit most planned features. Thicknesses are usually $1\frac{1}{2}$ and 2in. Thinner slabs than these should not be considered because they may well crack if subjected to a lot of traffic. Hexagonals and half-hexagonals come in 18in and 24in modules, and octagonals similarly, in 18in sizes. One of my favourites is the circular paving which forms intriguing stepping stones in my lawn. It can also be incorporated in a patio or large paved area with other stones and the awkward gaps filled in with pebbles. The latter are very useful for adding unusual design touches but should be placed carefully so that they are not used for the actual walking areas as they can be a little dangerous. Unfortunately they are not readily available, but a few specialist firms such as Teakle can supply. Carriage can be very costly over long distances.

In the more expensive slab ranges there are the exposed aggregate finishes. Berkshire flint and black basalt are offered, for example, by one or two specialist firms such as Bradstone. This firm also offers radius paving, a very useful type that enables the gardener to make paved circles, part circles, and paths that weave their way attractively through the garden.

Very nice paths can be made from crazy paving, which is readily obtainable from most garden centres and nurseries. Sometimes the local council will sell off their collection of broken paving slabs and these are very good value because they are usually quite thick.

Chippings

It is possible to make paths and drives from special cold asphalt which is available in 1cwt and $\frac{1}{2}$cwt bags. It is a very quick and simple way of doing this work as the material is simply tipped out of the bag, raked level to an approximate depth of $\frac{1}{2}$in and then rolled firm. Two colours are available, black and brown. The former has an approximate covering capacity of 20sq ft per cwt and the latter, 18sq ft. Special granite chippings are provided with the black material and this adds an attractive pattern to the surface when rolled in.

This type of path is only successful if it is made on top of a solid foundation. To key the material to non-absorbent surfaces, a special primer is available. A firm such as Expandite can supply this type of path-making material.

WALLING MATERIALS

There is plenty of colour in the modern walling stones and in very attractive shades such as pink, light grey, dark grey, York stone (a brown colour), slate blue, lilac, yellow, lavender and red.

The type of face or surface determines the overall effect of the finished wall. Most bricks or blocks have a rough or textured face, and some produce a 3-D effect with their pitched fall. On these the front face projects quite appreciably and the joints or bonds in the wall are therefore much more pronounced. Split stone walling is another type of block which has a very attractive rough texture to its face.

Stone sizes (in inches) range approximately as follows: $2\frac{1}{2} \times 12$, $5\frac{1}{2} \times 12$, $8\frac{1}{2} \times 12$, $8\frac{5}{8} \times 11\frac{5}{8}$, $5\frac{5}{8} \times 17\frac{5}{8}$, $4\frac{1}{8} \times 17\frac{5}{8}$, $2\frac{5}{8} \times 17\frac{5}{8}$, $2\frac{5}{8} \times 8\frac{3}{4}$, 18×2. Most bricks or blocks are 4–$4\frac{1}{2}$in wide (a measurement also referred to as the bed of the brick or stone). The bricks are laid with the textured face exposed. One slight difficulty is that some of these units have smooth ends so it is necessary to chip these off to provide a rough or textured face at the corners of walls. Special tops or coping stones can be purchased to add the finishing touches to the wall.

There is a way of building walls very quickly and without the bother of detailed bonding. This is to use special blocks of rough faced stone, each the equivalent of four or five pieces of random masonry. Returned blocks solve the problem of turning corners and constructing pillars or piers. These blocks or units are made from reconstituted Cotswold stone. The makers are Edwin Bradley Ltd.

Screen walling can be obtained in various pretty patterns or open-work designs. Most blocks are just under 12 × 12in so that by the time a mortar joint of about $\frac{3}{8}$in has been made, the modules are 12in square. This makes the task of quantity calculation more accurate. The blocks are generally $3\frac{5}{8}$–4in wide.

This type of walling needs supporting at intervals when it is more than 6ft in length and over 4ft in height. This is neatly done by pillars or pilasters as they are technically termed. These are specially designed hollow blocks with appropriate slots at the sides to receive the ends of the screen wall blocks. Special corner units are available also. The interior of these blocks is filled with concrete and reinforcing wire or steel rod as necessary. To finish off this type of walling, coping can be used for the wall tops and the tops of the pillars.

Walling has a special function in the sloping garden which has been levelled in 'steps'. An attractive wall both enhances the layout and, at the same time, holds back the banks of soil produced during the levelling operations. For steps leading from one level to another a combination of walling and paving is necessary. Mixed paving (both in size and colour) will add considerably to the appearance of such a feature and there is no reason why cavity walls cannot be used as retaining walls to provide the gardener with planting places.

CHAPTER 20

Greenhouses

A new world of plants is opened to the person who installs a greenhouse in his garden. He also provides himself with a very comfortable place to garden in, warm and sheltered from cold winds. Here also he has more control over his plants because he can provide the growing conditions, especially with regard to temperatures and watering. A greenhouse is in fact an investment in endless hours of absorbing interest and pleasure, and no one can really put into words the thrill of opening the greenhouse door and walking into that wonderful growing atmosphere which only a greenhouse can provide.

SITING

Before any attempt is made to select a greenhouse the site for it must receive very careful consideration. It must receive the maximum amount of sunlight, especially in the winter, and so must be kept well away from shadows from trees, fences or other obstructions. It must be sheltered from cold prevailing winds and should not be erected where it is unduly exposed to the battering of the occasional gale. My garden is only about a mile and a half from the sea on the south coast and I am very glad that I have sited my greenhouse in the lower part of the garden. We receive at least two severe gales per year and as yet no damage has been caused. But a very low-lying or badly drained position is no good either—it would either became waterlogged or a frost-pocket, possibly both on occasions!

The structure should be as close as is convenient to the house so that the costs of laying electricity cable or water to the greenhouse from the dwelling house is kept to the minimum. There is a lot to be said for having a lean-to design for this purpose. Unless the greenhouse is highly automated, it will be necessary to pay frequent visits to it for attending to the plants and adjusting the ventilators.

It must be admitted, however, that some greenhouses do not look at their best after a few seasons' use, and sometimes they become a dumping ground for all the odds and ends in the garden and quickly look very unsightly—especially if they are entirely of glass and everything is in view. If the gardener therefore wishes to conceal his greenhouse without depriving it of its valuable light source he can place it well beyond a dividing screen of some description or keep it in the vegetable garden if this is away from the house. Far better, however, to have an attractive design conveniently close to the house—and keep it tidy!

On any site, a good solid foundation is essential, and this is a low brick or concrete wall. Textured walling bricks are excellent for the construction of greenhouse bases, and if coloured stone is used a very attractive greenhouse siting can be achieved. Some greenhouse manufacturers provide, at extra cost, suitable interlocking concrete blocks, or something similar, as foundations for their own structures.

SIZES AND STYLES

Such is the diversity of greenhouse design that after you have read through a collection of manufacturers' catalogues you are probably more confused than ever before!

Cost will, as always, play a major part in decision-making, but when you purchase a greenhouse do get one which is slightly larger than you require immediately. More often than not the enthusiasm of the new greenhouse owner is such that he fills the available space at once and never ceases to regret that he did not buy just those extra few feet of staging (but see page 182 on extension units for metal designs). A length of 8ft should be considered as the minimum requirement; 10ft is ideal for average requirements. Similarly an 8ft width provides much more freedom of movement than the 6ft width of the smaller models. Ample headroom, especially at the eaves, is very useful also—don't forget that you will spend quite a lot of time at the staging. Height can, of course, be added by building the base a few inches higher in the initial setting work.

It is impossible to list all the sizes available but I think the following example of the permutations for just *one* cedarwood model will give some idea of the tremendous range. The first measurement is the width and the second the length: 4ft 6in × 6ft 3in; 6ft 6in × 6ft 6in, × 8ft, × 9ft 6in, and × 11ft; 8ft 2in × 8ft, × 9ft 6in, × 11ft, × 12ft 6in, × 16ft, × 19ft, × 22ft and × 25ft. In the 4ft 6in widths, the eaves are 5ft high and the ridge 6ft 6in; in the 6ft 6in widths, the eaves are 4ft 2in and the ridge 6ft 11in; and in the largest width of 8ft 2in the eaves are 4ft 6in and the ridge 7ft 5in.

In the wooden ranges there are several variations in style. Some models have glazing right down to ground level; some have low wooden sides; and some have all-glass fronts and three low wooden sides. The all-glass models admit maximum light and permit the culture of crops at ground level. Wooden-sided houses must have staging at glass level on which plants are grown. All-glass models lose heat more quickly than those which have the insulation of the lower boarding and are, therefore, more costly to heat.

There are a few models which are designed for erection on brick walls some 2–3ft high. These are the warmest of houses because of the high insulation properties of the brickwork.

Lean-to greenhouses are available in the all-glass, boarded or brick-wall types. These are easier and cheaper to heat than free-standing houses because they have the benefit of house warmth. They should be sited preferably on a warm, south-facing wall. The Dutch greenhouse is yet another type with its gently sloping sides. The glazing is done by sliding large sheets of glass into separate framelight-like sections, and requires no putty. These structures are quite attractive but glass replacement could be rather expensive.

One of the most interesting developments in greenhouses recently has been the remarkable break with tradition which just a few manufacturers have made. I am all for this and have been very surprised that it has taken such a long time to happen. These changes in design are sensible and practical ones too. I refer to the circular models which I will describe in more detail later on in the chapter.

METAL STRUCTURES

Cedarwood is at present perhaps the most popular material for greenhouse construction. It is attractive in appearance, though it needs occasional treatment if its colour is to be preserved—a task which is rather difficult on the glazing bars of a greenhouse. But it is a rot-proof timber and therefore a sound investment as far as longevity is concerned. Cedar is, however, getting expensive and it seems likely that aluminium will eventually take its place.

Aluminium is a most eye-catching metal when used for greenhouse construction and I, personally, think it the most attractive material for the new stylish designs. It is very durable and requires *no maintenance whatsoever*. This is a very important consideration to part-time gardeners.

There are two types of metal greenhouses—the aluminium and the steel structures. The latter is quite an attractive metal which must be well galvanised to be a good buying proposition, though even the best galvanising may eventually wear off in places and rust can be a slight problem. The galvanised steel structures cannot be considered completely maintenance-free as they require an occasional treatment with a suitable galvanised preparation.

Aluminium has produced the most exciting new shapes, such as the circular greenhouse, and this is because much more complex extensions or sections can be produced in metal. Despite this fact manufacturers of steel greenhouses have been rather conservative with their latest designs and failed to produce new shapes. Tradition dies hard in the gardening world, even though there are so many young new gardeners looking for new styles and modern applications of traditional materials. Several manufacturers of aluminium greenhouses have retained the standard shape while incorporating in the designs such innovations as doors that slide open or shut at the touch of a finger, and special extension units that can be quickly added to the existing greenhouse. These latter are an excellent feature. A small unit built on to the main greenhouse would provide a compact propagation section which could be heated to higher temperatures more economically; or you could have two separate greenhouses, one for low-temperatures and one for the more exotic subject that demand temperatures above 10°C (50°F).

I have had a great deal of pleasure from do-it-yourself aluminium kits. These are most satisfying to assemble and the finished product is handsome and well designed. Two firms specialise in these kits: Bast Glazing Clips who produce the Minibrite, and Edenlite who have a range of Eden models, with sliding doors and other special features. Both firms produce extension or add-on units. Ventilators can be placed at any position on the roof and extra ventilation is easily added.

Metal greenhouses in general possess one particularly useful feature and that is an extremely simple glazing system. This glass is placed on top of special glazing cord or rubber-like material and retained there by spring steel clips. Glazing time is reduced to an hour or so, depending on the size of the greenhouse, and repairs can be carried out very rapidly. Very little skill is required, and this system is much superior to the messy putty method which one still has to use for most wooden greenhouses.

The Hartley aluminium greenhouses have an unusual roof section sloped at several angles to catch the sun at all positions. These are in the de luxe range of aluminium designs, with very strong sections and a special coating over the aluminium. I should point out that, in order to provide additional strength, alloys are mixed with the aluminium and that strictly speaking all these greenhouses should be referred to as aluminium-alloy designs.

The circular aluminium greenhouses made by Humex, Whitehouse and Alexander are most unusal and eye-catching. They are the plantsman's ideal display house and are superb for special settings on the terrace or close to the dwelling house. When used in this way the greenhouse must be kept neat and well stocked because it is glazed to floor level and any untidiness is fully on view. The all-round staging which can be installed enables the user to display his pots to their fullest advantage. The only criticism I have of these circular greenhouses is that they can never be family affairs. There is room for only one person at a time, especially when all the staging is used. They are expensive of course, but quite a good investment where a greenhouse with a difference is required.

Steel greenhouses are stronger than the aluminium, but this in no way implies that aluminium structures are not strong —they are more than adequate for the average conditions experienced in the garden. But both steel and aluminium models suffer from condensation in cold weather and this can be a little troublesome in the unheated or low-temperature houses as it does add to the humidity or damp conditions. A lot can be done, however, to reduce the problem by sensible ventilation and, wherever possible, by putting up the heating.

In both types it is difficult to fix things inside, though most manufacturers provide small holes in parts of the framework so that training wires can be attached. The real difficulty arises when equipment has to be installed. This problem is reduced considerably in the Eden and Minibrite designs because special threaded bolts can be inserted in the extrusions inside the house and metal or wooden plates on which equipmen can be attached are then fixed to these.

Metal greenhouses have the minimum cross-sectioning in their construction and this means that there is slightly less light obstruction than in wooden greenhouses.

PLASTIC

The greenhouse of the future may well be made in its entirety from plastic or fibreglass. In these materials moulding of sweeps and curves is no problem and we should see beautiful shapes with graceful flowing lines. The structures would be completely maintenance-free and probably in a variety of pleasant colours. Heating elements could well be incorporated in the framework to give more working space and a more even heat distribution. Water pipes could likewise be integrated, with take-off points provided at certain places and spray heads or mist nozzles also built into the structure.

Coming down to earth as it were, plastics are already playing an important role as far as the greenhouse is concerned because there are designs available which are glazed in this material—the perfect solution to the problem of little boys and girls who throw stones! Replacement of damaged panels is reasonably cheap and easy. But plastic has a few disadvantages, among them quick loss of heat at night and the production of heavy condensation, which tends to fall on the plants below in large droplets unless the roof has a good pitch or slope. Sheet plastic also deteriorates through the action of sunlight, its life varying considerably according to thickness and quality. Some thin gauges may only last for two seasons whilst the thicker gauges may need replacement after 5–7 years. I must stress that these are *very* approximate figures.

For greater durability PVC materials should be considered. These are usually available in corrugated sections and for greenhouse work the clearest grade must be selected. Novolux, by ICI (Hyde), is one of the most sensible, and being available in large sheets, enables the glazing of a greenhouse to be done quite quickly. The supporting framework can be kept as simple as possible and need not be cut from very substantial timber, although the roof sections should be able to support the weight of snow and ice.

UNUSUAL DESIGNS

In this section we look at greenhouses that are slightly more complex in design. Oakworth greenhouses, for example, are constructed of oak and wire. The shape and size are quite conventional but the method by which the main framework of oak is strengthened internally by wire bracing is certainly unusual. The resulting rigid structure is excellent in exposed areas, where gardens may be subjected to frequent fierce winds and heavy falls of snow and ice.

There is something to be said for a combined shed and greenhouse design. Some models have the greenhouse part running down the length of the structure with the shed section in the other half. Other designs have the shed section at one gable end and the greenhouse section at the other.

The combined unit saves space and provides flexibility of working area. The shed section can be used not only for the storing but also the filling of pots and boxes, and for jobs such as seed sowing, pricking out and repotting without encroaching on valuable staging space. Remember that the greenhouse part needs all the sunlight.

Another unorthodox type is the free-standing lean-to greenhouse. This is an ordinary lean-to design with a solid back of wood, and is useful where, for some reason or other, it is not possible to erect a lean-to design against a wall. Usually the height to the ridge at the back of the structure is between 7ft 1in and 7ft 11in. Park Lines specialise in these and the shed/greenhouse models.

Sometimes a siting problem may be extremely difficult to overcome. There is, for instance, a greenhouse specially designed to take full advantage of all possible light on sites with very limited space, as for instance on the south side of a fence or a hedge. This is virtually a three-quarter span house with a very short span of roof on one side. The design is made by C. H. Whitehouse.

An unusual range of greenhouses is made by Messenger. They are all constructed from Western Red cedar and have a special ventilation system consisting of long roof ventilators and sliding ventilators in the low boarded base, ensuring extremely efficient air circulation.

There is a circular wooden greenhouse on the market. This is a six-sided design which is made by C. H. Whitehouse with sliding door and base ventilators. An automatic ventilator is also provided in the centre of the roof. It is about 8ft 8in from corner to corner and is in my opinion one of the most attractive of the circular designs. Being constructed of cedar it harmonises well with the garden surrounds, and yet it is stylish enough to be erected quite close to the dwelling house. Women, I am sure, will be delighted with this type of greenhouse and with the aluminium circular models. They are good to look at, compact, and quite easy to manage.

Another interesting range, made by Banbury, has concrete panels forming three side walls. These are finished in a rough textured face and on some designs these can be interchanged with the glass panels of the fourth wall so that light can be admitted to ground level on the sunniest side. Other models have concrete panels on all four sides. This range also has a unique ventilation system which allows a very good air movement inside the greenhouse, adjustable louvred panels being provided at the foot of the door and similar louvres at the far gable end. There is an unusually generous height at the eaves which provides the gardener with more working room.

Finally, there are new all-plastic bubble houses which are kept rigid or inflated by an electrically driven fan.

CHAPTER 21

Fitting Out the Greenhouse

The purchase of a greenhouse is quite an occasion, and its fitting out can be an even more exciting prospect especially now that quite a high standard of automation can be achieved for a relatively modest outlay.

The buying of equipment should commence with the basics; more sophisticated fittings can be added in stages. This is the best way to go about it if you are a beginner. As you gain experience and confidence your equipment can keep pace with your progress.

The development in greenhouse equipment has been quite remarkable during the past few years, particular progress being made in watering and propagation. Much of the new equipment which the grower uses to such good purpose these days is virtually scaled-down commercial apparatus.

BASIC EQUIPMENT

Staging in my opinion is the first thing to get, assuming that you are starting off with an unheated greenhouse. A place is necessary for pots and boxes and also to work on. Whether you install wooden or metal staging it *must* be substantial because staging has to support considerable loads and stresses. A few boxes or pots filled with soil are surprisingly heavy.

Most of the greenhouse manufacturers sell staging as an extra accessory. Cedar wood is frequently used, but if ordinary softwoods are employed the timber must be *thoroughly* treated with a wood preservative. Metal staging is sold by most of the aluminium greenhouse firms and the designs are attractive as well as functional.

Removable staging makes for versatility in a greenhouse, allowing the beds at ground level to be used, for example, for tomato and cucumber cultivation. Where deep wooden or brick sides are part of the greenhouse design, the staging can be a more permanent affair although it should be possible to move it easily for general maintenance work. For the enthusiastic pot plant grower, tiered staging can be purchased in the form of steps so that the plants can be arranged to their best advantage.

A watering can is another basic piece of equipment. Several sizes or capacities are available but for general greenhouse work a can of ½–1 gallon capacity should be selected, with a long spout so that plants can be reached at the back of the staging. Plastic cans are light and quite strong. Two roses should be obtained—a medium type and a fine one, the latter for the watering of seeds and seedlings because its fine spray does not damage tender plants or work soil away. Some cans are sold in very complete packs with two roses and a pot watering spout.

A selection of pots and boxes will be required. It is impossible to suggest quantities because personal requirements vary so much. Plastic types are durable, easy to clean, and light in weight on the staging. Standard plastic seed trays measure some 15 × 9in and are 2in deep. Smaller ones can be obtained, 8¾ × 6½ × 2in, and these are ideal as seed propagators. Deeper trays, 10 × 10 × 3in will be required for pricking out.

It is necessary to have a range of pot sizes—3 or 3½in, 4½ and 6in—so that plants in various stages of growth can be potted. A few 8in pots may be necessary for vigorous subjects in their final flowering pot size. For ring culture a considerable saving of money can be achieved if 9in diameter composite bottomless pots are used. Whilst on the subject of money-saving ideas, the heavy bituminised paper pots are well worth investigating. They last for a season or two and are light to handle and very easy to store.

It is essential to know what you have sown or planted and when, so a selection of wooden or metal labels will be required. The aluminium type last for years and can be marked so easily (see page 83).

I would recommend the purchase of just one piece of automatic equipment in this basic collection. This is a ventilator opener which requires no electricity or other form of power to operate it. A cam is operated by a piston-like system which in turn is activated by a temperature-sensitive oil inside the piston. Usually the ventilator opener starts to open at a temperature of approximately 16°C (60°F). One unit fixed to a ventilator in the roof will ensure that some movement of air will be provided whilst the owner is away. It is a piece of equipment that will solve a lot of holiday problems! They are quite expensive at about £6–£8 each but are very easy to fix.

HEATING

The unheated greenhouse can provide a great deal of interest and pleasure but it is difficult to make much use of it during the cold winter months. If some form of heating can be supplied, the range of plants which can be grown increases considerably and so does the enjoyment.

The type of heating and the temperatures required depend on the amount of money that can be spared and the estimated running costs. The temperature range available will determine which plants can be grown successfully.

The newcomer would be well advised to progress slowly and start his heating at the lower range of 7°C (45°F). This provides adequate frost protection and sufficient warmth to keep plants growing slowly, but it does not produce a dry atmosphere so care must be taken to see that some ventilation is given on favourable occasions.

A rise in temperature to 10°C (50°F) reduces dampness and provides a much better growing atmosphere. It should be appreciated, however, that even this small increase adds a great deal to the running costs. To maintain a temperature of 7°C (45°F) would cost approximately 50p per week for a 8 × 10 × 6ft greenhouse. Raise this temperature to 10°C (50°F) and the running costs leap up to 95p per week! These figures are for electrical heating. The cheapest form of heating is paraffin oil, next comes solid fuel, and the most expensive is electricity. The cost of the actual apparatus also runs in that order.

The next consideration is convenience. This is where the order is practically reversed. There is no doubt that electricity scores highly, especially as no other form of heating can at present provide such a degree of automation. Thermostatic control ensures that the desired temperature is maintained by the automatic switching on and off. A certain amount of automation is provided with a paraffin heater if the Cooper-Walker Module is purchased. This has a rod-type thermostat which controls the flow of fuel to a special burner. Some solid fuel boilers also have a system of temperature control. The Metomatic boiler by the Metallic Construction Co (Derby) has a controller which closes or opens the air inlet according to the temperature of the water returning along the bottom pipe.

The cheapest apparatus to install is the paraffin heater. Next comes the solid fuel apparatus with its pipes, stands, and boiler. Some of the latest boilers require no shed or covering and can be left out in the open. I prefer to keep mine covered to preserve its life and to use the small shed-like structure which houses it as a nice dry place for the garden footwear!

Electric heating is quite expensive to install chiefly because the work *must* be undertaken by *qualified* electricians. The special mains cable which carries the power from the mains in the dwelling house to the greenhouse is very expensive, and whether it is carried overhead or is buried safely below ground level must depend on the ruling of the local authorities. Waterproof or damp-proof electrical fittings are absolutely necessary for the greenhouse and these also are expensive. The heating apparatus itself is relatively expensive also and essential extras such as a rod thermostat are not cheap. It is as well to look on the installation of electricity in the greenhouse as a good investment, and if extra plug sockets are installed while you are about it, and a sufficiently high loading of mains cable allowed for future developments, the adding of extra electrical equipment from time to time will be an easy task.

There are several types of electrical heating apparatus available. Tubular heaters made from aluminium are about 2in in diameter and are available in lengths of 2–16ft, and usually with a loading of 60 watts per foot run. They can be attached most conveniently to the sides of the greenhouse in single rows or in banks; they are not in the way and look very neat. They should be connected to a suitable thermostat.

Fan heaters are the most efficient for even and thorough heat distribution. The warmed air is gently wafted to all the far corners of the greenhouse, and in the summer the heating element can be cut out and the fan used to create air circulation. The fan movement of air is particularly helpful in minimising damp conditions.

The power or rating of a heater has to be considered when a selection is being made. This is in kilowatts (kW) and the ratings range from about 1½kW to 3kW. Many leading manufacturers provide brochures which give easy-to-use calculations for determining the correct size of heater to buy. Where these details are not available in printed form most firms will be pleased to advise, or the local sundries firm or garden centre will help.

Care needs to be taken over the choice of a thermostat for electrical heating appliances. For the most accurate control, the aspirated type cannot be bettered. This virtually 'samples' the air continuously and maintains a very close control. Next in accuracy comes the rod-type and finally the hand operated models. Built-in thermostats are standard with most fan-heaters (others can have an external thermostat attached) and temperature settings are made via a knob which is turned to the required temperature number or mark.

A separate thermostat should be positioned carefully so that it is not affected by direct sunlight, and a little shade or cover over it should be provided. It must not be placed in direct draught. One of the best positions for it is a few feet from the far gable end from the door and about 8in away from the roof glass. A place about halfway down one side of the roof would give an average condition of the greenhouse air temperature.

At the time of writing I am involved with the development of a gas greenhouse heater which, if successful (and there are all the signs that it could be) will be a tremendous break-through in greenhouse heating. Not only will this heater provide for accurate automation but running costs could be much lower than for electricity. In fact, it looks as though the amateur can heat at temperatures of 10–13°C (50–60°F) for less than it would cost to heat with electricity at 7°C (45°F). The heater would be quite compact and little or no maintenance would be required. It would be suitable only for North Sea gas as it has no chimney and should burn without any trace of fume damage!

WARMING CABLES

The soil in borders can be warmed by special cables which

are laid on the bottom of the border and covered with about 6in of soil. An increase in soil temperature of between 6–12°C (10–20°F) above air temperature can be maintained with a loading of between 6 and 8 watts per sq ft.

The same type of cable can be used to make up a propagator on the greenhouse staging. A box or casing containing a 2in layer of builder's sand is laid on the staging. The warming cable is then laid carefully in the sand and a further 2in of sand placed on top. Pots or boxes of seeds are placed on the sand and peat is carefully placed in between to retain the bottom heat. Temperatures of about 12–18°C (20–30°F) above air temperature will be required, needing a loading of between 10 and 12 watts per sq ft. Special thermostats inserted in the medium will ensure accurate temperatures and low running costs. These cables can be used for outdoor frames also.

A combination of soil and air warming cables can be installed in a home-made greenhouse propagator to provide an excellent place for the raising of plants from seeds and cuttings. Running costs can be as low as 5 to 7½p or so per week.

Specialist greenhouse heating firms, eg Humex, Camplex, House and Garden Automation, and Autogrow, can supply complete package deals in this type of heating arrangement. The equipment is neat and fairly compact. All parts are carefully designed to provide the highest safety standard, which is so vital.

SHADING

Unfortunately there seems to have been little progress made in automatic shading, apart from the electric motors devised by Humex. These wind or unwind a lath-type exterior blind up and down the roof. One drawback to automation in this field is that it is very expensive and market potential is small.

Spring-loaded green plastic roller shades, fitted inside the greenhouse roof, provide a simple and reasonably effective system which the amateur can well afford. They can be adjusted quickly to any position to suit the sun's angle, but I find that they build up the temperature inside the house in hot weather and seem to reduce the effectiveness of ventilation.

Proprietary shading preparations like Summer Cloud can be sprayed lightly on the external roof glass and if a faint speckling is achieved a very effective shade is provided. It is a trifle messy, however, and tends to coat the framework of the house and is difficult to remove.

I have found the use of very fine Netlon greenhouse shading mesh one of the best methods. It is made from strong plastic material and can be pinned to the undersides of the roof bars. In metal houses attachment is a problem, but it could be draped over horizontal wires run along the roof. It can be removed very quickly and should last for many seasons. As it is a mesh the air moves freely through it and quite a cool atmosphere can be maintained.

VENTILATION

Very few greenhouse manufacturers supply sufficient of this in their designs. You cannot have too much ventilation, but it is very difficult to increase the number of ventilators in the standard wooden and metal designs. The exceptions are the Eden and Minibrite models where extra vents can be purchased and installed in a very short time without disturbing the structure.

An automatic ventilator opener, or several, would solve holiday problems and reduce attention to the house during the day. One fixed to a roof ventilator and another to a side ventilator would ensure a good flow of air throughout the greenhouse (see page 190).

Another method of changing the air regularly and thus cooling the interior is to use ventilating or extractor fans powered by electricity. They are usually fixed in the far gable end and when connected to a rod thermostat, will begin to operate at the set temperature. As a general rule about thirty air changes per hour are required. A fan with an impeller of $7\frac{1}{2}$in diameter is suitable for greenhouses of up to 280cu ft. For up to 500cu ft an impeller of 9in is required, and for up to 1,000cu ft a 12in diameter would be necessary. A roof-mounted model is available from Camplex. For the small greenhouse the Guardian fan is very useful. This does not extract air but simply causes a gentle turbulence which prevents stagnant air conditions. Running night and day, this little 8in diameter fan costs only approximately 4p per week!

A new conception in ventilation comes from House and Garden Automation. This is a large fan which draws in air from outside the greenhouse and then blows it along lengths of perforated pipe arranged down the greenhouse. Quite a good cooling effect is achieved. This system will probably be developed still further and a lot of exciting new pieces of equipment may well result. The same fan can be used to heat the greenhouse when a heating element is installed and warm air can be blown through the ventilator ducts or pipes.

WATERING

Automation is playing an important part in easing the burden of this essential operation, and also in helping the gardener to obtain better growing results from regular watering.

Tray and trickle systems

The simplest and cheapest form of watering is the capillary tray. This is a plastic or fibreglass container with a water reservoir in its base. A second tray fits inside this larger one and holds the sand. Water rises into the sand tray via a special wick or feed hole and the sand is maintained in a suitably moist condition. Pot plants placed on the sand draw their individual water requirements from this moisture. This is the Camplex System. Refilling with water will be necessary about once every 10–14 days.

Another tray system is available from Humex. These trays are filled with sand and have a small water reservoir at one side. The tray is fed with water via a 1 gallon jar connected to it by a small bore plastic tube. This rather limits the amount of automation because the bottle needs replenishing at least once a day. For full automation the tray can be linked to a plastic water tank with ball valve control. The tank is fed from the mains water supply and the ball valve arrangement allows automatic filling. Several trays can be linked together by short lengths of tubing. In this way the system can be extended as the finances allow. The trays are specially designed to fit on the standard greenhouse staging (2ft and 2ft 9in wide). Tray sizes are from 1ft 10in × 2ft 10in to 1ft 10in × 3ft 9in.

Another reasonably cheap watering system consists of a tank supplied by mains water and controlled by a ball valve. This feeds a trickle irrigation line some 23ft in length with twenty drip nozzles at 12in intervals. These nozzles can be regulated to provide various rates of water application. The line may be arranged along the soil border so that these nozzles water around individual plants or can be placed over pots to keep them nice and moist.

For the automatic watering of large areas, there is a system which moistens a complete staging. Ordinary staging is converted to hold about 2in of sand, and special 'feeding' units are inserted at intervals through the bottom of the staging and connected to a device which maintains a correct level of water in the bottom of these feeder units. The device is, in turn, connected to a large tank of water and this can be connected to the main water supply and controlled by a ball-valve.

The sand is kept primed with water and is always in a damp condition. Pot plants placed on the sand absorb this moisture and the compost in the pots is maintained in a suitably moist condition. If clay pots are used it will be necessary to insert a short length of glass wool or cotton wick through the drainage hole and bury the other end of it in the sand. This draws up the moisture from the sand into the pot. Because plastic pots have such a thin wall, they are in much closer contact to the sand and if pushed into the surface gently a really good contact is made.

These systems require no electrical power and are, therefore ideal for the greenhouse owner who has not or cannot have an electrical supply. For those who can install electricity there are more sophisticated devices available.

Electrically controlled systems

British Overhead Irrigation have developed a solar controlled automatic watering package deal which provides the following watering systems: a humidification nozzle to be mounted in the greenhouse ridge for automatic damping down; two overhead spray nozzles for the watering of small plants, seed boxes and seedlings (these cover an area of about 16sq ft); a mist propagation jet head which provides an exceptionally fine mist or drift of water over cuttings (to cover a propagating bench 3 × 3ft); and ten trickle nozzles mounted in a small bore flexible pipe for watering individual pot plants or plants in the border. The 'brain' of this unit is a solar controller which reacts to daylight and triggers off the watering operations in bursts of about 5 seconds' duration. The stronger the light the more frequent the watering. The solar unit can also be set by hand to vary the frequency.

What is so useful about this system is the fact that it has a transformer which reduces the mains voltage to a very safe 24 volts. No skilled plumbing or electrical knowledge is necessary to set it up. I have used this system in one of my greenhouses and commend it especially to the woman gardener because it is easy to use, makes life a lot easier when a host of other gardening routine tasks have to be carried out, and gives her a chance to try her hand at plant propagation.

There are one or two other mist watering and propagation systems available to the amateur. One, also by British Overhead Irrigation known as the BOIL system, employs a transformer which reduces the mains electricity voltage to 24 volts. An electronic 'leaf' or moisture detector controls the frequency of the mist burst. When the electrodes are covered with moisture the electrical contact is broken and the mist application turned off. Once the electrodes dry out through evaporation the current is turned on and watering starts again. A commendable feature of this detector is that the carbon electrodes are replaceable. An atomiser jet is mounted on a short pipe and a solenoid valve is also provided which shuts the water on and turns it off when signalled by the solenoid.

Another mist propagation system is made by Humex and this is powered by mains voltage electricity. Similar mist heads are available but the detector or 'leaf' works on a simple balance principle. One arm of the detector carries an absorbent pad, the other a low voltage contact. The pad absorbs moisture as the cuttings are sprayed and becomes heavier and eventually tips the arm. As this happens, the low voltage contact is broken and the water supply is switched off. Moisture gradually evaporates from the pad, which becomes lighter and rises. Contact is made, the water is switched on and the cuttings are coated once again with an extremely fine mist of water.

PROPAGATORS

The successful propagation of seeds depends on the provision of a high temperature. This can be very costly if the whole of the greenhouse is heated but surprisingly cheap for only a limited area. This heated area is the propagator, usually consisting of a large tray or base with a glass or plastic tap or dome.

Several sizes are available and most requirements can be satisfied. For the very small greenhouse where only a few seeds at a time are raised, the one-seed-box-capacity propagator is very useful. The unit consists of a base plate which is heated and small feet support the seed box a few inches above its surface. A clear plastic cover is supplied which fits over the seed box and provides extra protection. A larger version takes two standard seed trays. Running costs are about 5 to 6½p per week.

I should make it clear at this stage that a protective dome is necessary if a seed raiser is going to be used in an unheated greenhouse. The gentle heat provided by the base plate is not sufficient to give air protection against frost or very low temperatures inside the greenhouse, and the cover ensures that this warmth is contained around the plants and not allowed to escape into the surrounding air.

For more ambitious requirements the larger capacity propagators will be necessary. These hold about four standard seed boxes or trays, or seven 4in pots, or fifteen 6in pots. The base of the propagator is made of glass fibre and the whole thing is quite deep to give the young seedlings plenty of headroom. The top of the propagator is covered with three slats of glass which can be adjusted to supply ventilation. A large perspex dome can be purchased as a useful extra to turn the propagator into a miniature greenhouse where pot plants can be grown to maturity—calceolarias, for instance, which require temperatures of about 10°C (50°F) minimum for success.

This propagator is heated by means of special soil warming cables buried in the base material. A rod thermometer is built in the base to provide automatic temperature control, and is usually set between 10–20°C (50–70°F). This form of control also ensures extremely low running costs and for only about 10p per week, a temperature of 16°C (60°F) can be maintained! Firms such as Camplex, Humex and Autogrow are specialists in the manufacture of greenhouse propagators.

OTHER USEFUL ACCESSORIES

Sterilisers

Clean soil, free from disease or pest infection is important and a small electric steriliser could be a good investment. A capacity of ½–1cu ft is sufficient and as the soil can be completely sterilised in 1–1½ hours, several batches can be dealt with in a day if necessary. Powered by electricity, the units are very neat and efficient. They are available from Camplex.

I prefer to sterilise my soil by steam because this is much quicker and results in a moister soil; the previously mentioned sterilisers are very good but they can dry the soil out. The Nobles steam unit is of ½cu ft capacity and is virtually a bucket with perforated base. The bucket part which holds the soil, is placed on top of a small container of water. An automatic electric element heats the water and soil is treated in approximately 10 minutes.

Control panel

A waterproof control panel which neatly contains all the vital switches, plug sockets and fuses for the electrical equipment in the greenhouse is an accessory which should be installed by a competent electrician. But once installed it enables the amateur to connect up various pieces of electrical equipment easily, safely and very quickly, simply by attaching a suitable earthed and fused plug to the cable and plugging it into the control box.

Maximum–minimum thermometer

A thermometer that registers the highest and lowest temperatures inside the greenhouse is invaluable as a check on the efficiency of the heating equipment and the accuracy of the thermostat. Latest models have a push-button resetting device.

Lighting

Special greenhouse lighting is available for extending day-light hours so that chrysanthemums and other flowers can be grown out of season—bud and flower formation is regulated by length of daylight. Special irradiator types must be used and the red ratio of the light spectrum is important; one made by Camplex has a red ratio of 12 per cent. These lights can be hung from the roof of the greenhouse to illuminate plants on the staging, but for safety's sake only specially designed units, sealed against the entry of damp or water which could make them extremely dangerous, should be used.

CHAPTER 22

Sheds and Other Things

The efficiency of equipment depends to a great extent on the way in which it is stored. Tools in orderly rows are always at hand and no time is lost searching for the always vanishing secateurs and hand trowels! Tools stored in a dry, airy place will not rust as badly as those left around in damp places. Mechanical equipment especially must be kept as dry as possible, especially electrical parts.

The ideal storage place is a shed and you should have no trouble in finding exactly the right size for your requirements. There are the miniature sheds for the allotment or the very tiny garden, large enough to take a small mower and a collection of basic garden tools such as spade, fork, hoe, rake etc.

The average popular model is about 6–8ft long and 6ft wide and this is sufficient to accommodate most collections of garden equipment with enough space left over for a useful bench. Sheds of 15–16ft long are ideal if you have lots of bulky equipment.

DESIGNS AND BUYING POINTS

It was only fairly recently that some manufacturers decided it was time to change shed design, and thank goodness they have done so because the average garden shed was not a thing of beauty! What a difference a flat roof makes, and deep facia boards, not to speak of the large picture windows and the welcome extra light they admit. Coloured panels add considerable charm to the appearance of some of these new designs.

I have one complaint about most shed designs, including some of the modern ones, and it is that insufficient ventilation is provided. An extra pound or so would surely remedy this. A shed heats up considerably in very warm weather and needs a good flow of air. In damp weather, movement of air inside does much to reduce condensation and general dampness.

Check to see that the main framing is substantial. In some designs the main supports are cut from the thinnest section of timber the manufacturers dare use. Avoid these, especially where weak timber is found in the roof sections. Remember that the roof may have to support quite a weight of snow or ice and a sagging roof will leak badly in time. Sheds erected in exposed gardens will receive severe buffeting from time to time and unless they are strongly made there will soon be gaps between panels or spaces opening up in vital joints. Where there are gaps there will be draughts and bad leaks.

One or two designs are superbly strong and not too expensive either, the main framework being made from timber 2in sq. For generous timber sizes I always feel that the few extra pounds outlay are well worth it.

Several manufacturers provide a generous door width and this is an important buying point where bulky equipment such as mowers has to be manoeuvred through the doorway.

Whether to have cedar or softwood is another point to consider. The former will not rot or warp but is much more expensive and some of the prices for such sheds are a little excessive for what you get. The cedar is only a quite thin outer cladding, and most of the inner framework is made from ordinary softwoods.

A softwood cladded shed must be treated against rot and creosote can be used for this purpose. It weathers to an attractive brown colour eventually and there is no doubt that this preparation preserves most efficiently. The copper napthenate products such as Cuprinol and Rentoprufe are excellent preservatives also and can be obtained in brown or green. The latter weathers to a rather pale green and personally I find it a little disappointing and a trifle insipid on large surfaces.

A wooden floor, which is well worth the extra cost, makes a much warmer and dryer place, especially if you want to use the shed as a do-it-yourself workshop. Particular care must be taken to provide good and adequate support for the floor joists so that there is no danger of the floor sagging. These floors have to take a lot of weight and considerable wear and tear; it is very difficult indeed to try to repair a faulty base once the shed is erected. The cheaper shed floors need particular care with supports as their joists are made from rather thin wood.

FITTINGS FOR THE SHED

Neat tool storage requires a range of suitable fittings. There are one or two rather ingenious models which, although fairly compact, will hold a large number of miscellaneous tools. Detachable hooks are the secret. They can be clipped to any position on the basic framework of the rack. One rack which is only 2ft 4in long and 6½in high can hold a large broom, rake, spade, fork, hoe, pair of shears and lawn rake. If several of these racks are fixed along the shed walls a large collection of miscellaneous tools can be stored very neatly.

Wire frame tool racks or shelves are available for holding small tools. They are also excellent for drying bulbs, tubers etc before storage. Some tool racks have a clip-on shelf which adds to their usefulness.

A work bench or even some greenhouse staging would be a useful accessory for the shed. Either would provide a most useful storage area especially for pots and boxes. The shed staging could be used for the filling of seed boxes or pots and if seed sowing, pricking out and potting could also be carried out here it would leave more room in the greenhouse.

If the shed is sited reasonably close to the dwelling house, there is no reason why an electricity supply could not be taken there to provide lighting or perhaps some heating. Or if the greenhouse is already supplied with electricity, a branch supply could be taken from there to the shed. An electric heater set at a low temperature would maintain a drying atmosphere and provide frost protection for plant tubers etc stored in the shed.

BITS AND PIECES

Here in this last section are all those odd items of gardening equipment which we have not mentioned elsewhere.

Take gloves for example. I find that I cannot get on with gloves when I garden, nor can my wife, but I do appreciate the fact that they keep the hands clean and prevent those odd cuts and knocks one can receive during many gardening operations. The only time I welcome a pair of stout gloves is when I have a lot of rose pruning to do! The leather gauntlet types are ideal for these occasions and those with a deep cuff should be selected to protect the wrists. There are styles to suit both men and women.

Specially for women are several fancy types of glove with gay floral patterns; they are lightweight and waterproof. For protection against corrosive spraying materials etc, I recommend the liquid repellent types made from good heavy-duty material. Vinyl-impregnated cotton is made up into useful all purpose gloves, available in men's and women's sizes.

A garden apron is quite a good idea especially if it has bib and pocket in which secateurs or other small hand tools can be slipped. It is especially useful when working with soil and pots in the greenhouse.

Suitable footwear is a high priority item on my list because feet can get so cold or damp, especially in the winter period.

Cloggees are one answer to this problem. They are strong, resilient PVC garden shoes, fully lined with a comfortable inner sole. They are fairly light to wear and can be slipped on or off very quickly. No half-sizes are available but there is a wide fitting range of from 4 to 11.

The knees take a lot of punishment in garden operations. A great deal of work such as grass clipping, planting and weeding is done more comfortably in a kneeling position and special knee protectors can be obtained to ease the wear and tear. They are made from tough flexible rubber, quite light in weight and with a quick fastening device requiring no buckles or buttons. Better still is a kneeling stool, which conveniently turns the other way up to make a low seat. Robust tubular handles give support as one kneels down or gets up and I am sure that the elderly will find this type of stool a real treasure.

Ladders and stools for standing on are always needed—for reaching wall-trained plants, as an aid to pruning activities, for maintenance work on greenhouses or sheds and construction work on walls, pergolas etc.

A compost bin is a great help for the speedy rotting down of grass mowings, trimmings from the flower and vegetable borders and collected autumn leaves. The most efficient bins are those that allow the maximum amount of air to penetrate the heap, and I have found the wire mesh type the most successful. I particularly like the collapsible ones which are easily removed, once a large heap has been formed and rotted down, to take a new heap stacked close by. The Hago bin is of this type.

Some rubbish cannot be rotted down on the compost heap but has to be burnt. An incinerator affords the cleanest and quickest method of disposal, and here again I have found that the best design is one with open sides so that a really good draught is maintained. A substantial framework is necessary otherwise it also burns through fairly quickly.

Suppliers/Manufacturers of Garden Aids

Hand Tools

MULTIRAKE

Tudor Ltd, Hengoed, Glamorgan CF8 7XD, South Wales

SCRAKE

Spearwell Garden Tools Ltd (Spear & Jackson), St Paul's Rd, Wednesbury, Staffs

SWOE (hoe)

Wilkinson Sword Ltd (Colnbrook) Ltd, Sword Works, Southfield Road, London W4

TERREX SPADE

Wolf Tools for Garden & Lawn Ltd, Ross-on-Wye, Herefordshire

WOLF PUSH-PULL WEEDER

Wolf Tools for Garden & Lawn Ltd

WOLF HANDLE LENGTHS

Wolf Tools for Garden & Lawn Ltd

Mechanical Tools

COMPLETE POWER PACK

Landmaster (Ltd), Sterte Road, Poole BH15 2AF, Dorset

GARDENCARE
Farmfitters Ltd, Gt Haseley, Oxford OX9 7PF

HOWARD ROTAVATOR
Howard Rotavator Co Ltd, West Horndon, Essex

MERRY TILLER
Wolseley Engineering Ltd, Witton, Birmingham B6 7JA

Mowers and Lawn Care

AMBASSADOR
Hayters Ltd, Spellbrook, Bishop's Stortford, Herts

ATCO MOWERS
Charles H. Pugh Ltd, Atco Works, Tilton Road, Birmingham B9 4PR

AJAX
Ransomes Sims & Jefferies Ltd, Ipswich, Suffolk

BROTT
Portec (UK) Ltd, Vauxhall Industrial Estate, Ruabon, Wrexham, Denbighshire

CYCLONE
Andrews Ltd, The Garden Machine Centre, Sunningdale, Berks

GINGE
Ginge-Raadvad (UK) Ltd, 53 Culver Road, St Albans, Herts

HUSQVARNA
Hyett Adams Ltd, Stonehouse, Gloucestershire GL10 1BR

LLOYD PENNSYLVANIA
Lloyds of Letchworth Ltd, Letchworth, Herts

MOUNTFIELD
M3 & M5
G. D. Mountfield Ltd, East Street, Maidenhead SL6 8AN, Berks

QUALCAST
SUPERLITE
Qualcast (Lawn Mowers) Ltd, Sunnyhill Avenue, Derby DE3 7JT

SISIS
Sisis Equipment (Macclesfield) Ltd, Macclesfield SK10 2IZ, Cheshire

SUFFOLK SWIFT
Qualcast (Lawn Mowers) Ltd, Sunnyhill Avenue, Derby DE3 7JT

TORO
Flymo Ltd, Greycaine Road, Watford WD2 4PT, Herts

VICEROY Mk 2
Suffolk Ironfoundry Ltd, Sunnyhill Avenue, Derby DE3 7JT

WEBB WHIPPET
Webb Lawnmowers Ltd, Tame Road, Witton, Birmingham B6 7HP

WESTWOOD
Westwood Engineering Co Ltd, Fryers Works, Abercromby Avenue, High Wycombe, Bucks

WOLF CABLEFIX
Wolf Tools for Garden & Lawn Ltd

WOLF
ROTONDOR
Wolf Tools for Garden & Lawn Ltd

Pruning and Trimming

ANDREWS JENNY
Andrews Ltd, The Garden Machine Centre, Sunningdale, Berks

FELCO

Burton McCall & Co, 55 Welford Road, Leicester LE2 7AE

ROLCUT

Rolcut Ltd, Horsham, Sussex

TARPEN MINI-ENGINE

Tarpen Engineering Co Ltd, 7 Coronation Road, Park Royal, London NW10

Artificial Rain

GARDENA

Smith & Davis Ltd, Beacon Works, Friar Park Road, Wednesbury

GEECO

G. & E. Equipment and Contracts Ltd, Geeco Works, New Milton BH25 6SE

HAWS CANS

E. J. Woodman & Sons Ltd, High Street, Pinner, Middlesex

HOZELOCK

Hozelock Ltd, Haddenham, Aylesbury, Bucks

WOLF HOSE REEL

Wolf Tools for Garden & Lawn Ltd

Carrying

SUSSEX TRUG

E. J. Woodman & Sons, High Street, Pinner, Middlesex

TIMPERLEY FOLD-A-CART

Timperley Engineering (WPM) Ltd, Park Road, Timperley, Altrincham, Cheshire

Stop the Birds!

ULSTRON NETTING

E. J. Woodman & Sons (see *Carrying*)

Protected Cultivation

ACCESS FRAME

Access Frames, Crick, Rugby

Fighting the Foes

DUSTER

E. J. Woodman & Sons Ltd, High Street, Pinner, Middlesex

LOW-VOLTAGE SPRAYER

E. P. Barrus Ltd, 12-16 Brunel Road, London W3

SPRAYERS

Associated Sprayers Ltd, Birmingham B7 5SS

Water as a Garden Feature

FOUNTAINS, PLASTIC LINERS, PRE-FORMED POOLS (fish, plants, etc), PUMPS (Sealion, Big John, Little Giant, Otter),

Anglo Aquarium Plant Co Ltd, Wildwoods, Theobalds Park Road, Enfield, Middlesex

WATERFALLS

Highlands Water Gardens, Rickmansworth, Herts

Plant Containers

ASBESTOS-CEMENT

Urastone, Higham, Rochester, Kent

CONCRETE

Marley Concrete Ltd, Guildford, Surrey

CONTINENTAL

E. Christian & Co Ltd, 8-10 Shad Thames, London SE1

Patio Design Ltd, 4 Ladbroke Grove, Holland Park Avenue, London W11

GROWING CABINET

House and Garden Automation, 186 High Street, Barnet

INDOOR SELF-WATERING

Riviera, Simplex of Cambridge Ltd, Sawston, Cambridge

JARDINIERES

Hall & Goulding Ltd, Shripney Road, Bognor Regis, Sussex

TEAK TUBS

Lister Garden Furniture, R. A. Lister & Co Ltd, Dursley, Gloucestershire

WALL HOLDERS

Auriol (Guildford) Ltd, Trading Estate, Farnham, Surrey

Leisure in the Garden—Furniture

ALUMINIUM, WOOD, SWING HAMMOCK

E. Atkins Ltd, Atcraft Leisure Furniture, Atcraft Works, Ealing Road, Alperton, Wembley, Middlesex

CANE

Whines & Edgeler, The Bamboo People, Godmanstone, Dorchester, Dorset

IROKO, BRANSON, ALUMINIUM

L. E. Gant Ltd, Richmond, Surrey

METAL

A. E. (Metals) Ltd, Wood Lane, Birmingham 24

SWING HAMMOCKS AND OTHER DESIGNS

Farmfitters Ltd, St Haseley, nr Oxford

WOOD

Wrinch & Sons Ltd, St Lawrence Works, Ipswich

Summerhouses

Banbury Buildings Holdings Ltd, Robins House, Royal Leamington Spa, Warwickshire

F. Pratten & Co Ltd, Midsomer Norton, Bath BA3 4AG

Park Lines & Co, 717-719 Seven Sisters Rd, London N15

Robert H. Hall & Co (Kent) Ltd, Paddock Wood, Tonbridge, Kent

T. Bath & Co Ltd, PO Box 5, Tonbridge, Kent

Home Extensions

Banbury Buildings Holdings Ltd, Robins House, Royal Leamington Spa, Warwickshire

Blacknell Buildings Ltd, Pinehurst Avenue, Farnborough, Hampshire

Classic Portable Buildings Ltd, South Bridge Works, Brighton Road, Coulsdon, Surrey

Marley Concrete Ltd, Peasmarsh, Guildford, Surrey

Robert H. Hall & Co (Kent) Ltd (see *Summerhouses*)

T. Bath & Co Ltd (see *Summerhouses*)

Swimming Pools

Blue Line Pools, Daux Road, Billingshurst, Sussex

Capital Swimming Pools Ltd, The Bury Farm, Pednor Road, Chesham, Bucks

Cranleigh Products Ltd, Reading, Berks

Fernden Liner Pools Ltd, High Street, Godalming, Surrey

Gazelle Swimming Pools Ltd, Kingston House, Portsmouth Road, Thames Ditton, Surrey

Purley Pools Ltd, Godstone Road, Purley, Surrey

Rutherford Swimming Pools, Battle, Sussex

Garden Lighting

Denloy Products, Cordwallis Street, Maidenhead

Elsworthy Electronics Ltd, 27-31 Broadley Terrace, London NW1

Highlands Water Gardens, Rickmansworth, Herts

Proops Brothers Ltd, The Hyde Industrial Estate, Edgware Road, Hendon, London NW9 6JS

Barbecues

Continenta Ltd, 122 Ennerdale Road, Richmond on Thames

Garden Appliances Ltd, Thame Park Industrial Estate, Chinnor Road, Thame, Oxon

The Use of Stone—Paving and Walling

Expandite Ltd, Chase Road, London NW10

Edwin H. Bradley & Sons Ltd, Swindon, Wilts

Marley Concrete Ltd, Guildford, Surrey

Noelite Ltd, Borough Green, Kent

Redland Bricks Ltd, Graylands, Horsham, Sussex

S. Marshall & Sons, Ltd, Southowram, Halifax

W. Teakle & Co Ltd, 26 Denmark Street, Wokingham, Berks

Greenhouses

Alton Glasshouses Ltd, Alton Works, Bewdley, Worcestershire

Banbury Buildings Holdings Ltd (see *Summerhouses*)

C. H. Whitehouse Ltd, Buckhurst Works, Frant, Sussex

Crittall Manufacturing Co Ltd, Horticultural Dept, Braintree, Essex

Edenlite Ltd, Station Lane, Witney, Oxfordshire

F. Pratten & Co Ltd (see *Summerhouses*)

Hartley Clear Span Ltd, Greenfield, nr Oldham, Lancs

Humex Ltd, 5 High Road, Byfleet, Weybridge, Surrey

ICI (Hyde) Ltd, Newton Works, Hyde, Cheshire

L. J. Alexander, Rampore Nurseries, Paice Lane, Medstead, nr Alton, Hampshire

Messenger & Co Ltd, Cumberland Road, Loughborough

Minibrite Greenhouses, Bast Glazing Clips Ltd, Cambridge Road, Comberton, Cambridge

Park Lines & Co (see *Summerhouses*)

Robert H. Hall & Co Ltd (see *Home Extensions*)

T. Bath & Co Ltd (see *Summerhouses*)

Worth Buildings Ltd, Oakworth Division, Donnington, Wellington, Shropshire

Greenhouse Heating

ELECTRIC,
IN ALL FORMS

Autogrow Ltd, 3-13 Quay Road, Blyth, Northumberland

Camplex Products, Simplex Dairy Equipment Co Ltd, Horticultural Division, Sawston, Cambridge

House and Garden Automation, 186 High Street, Barnet

Humex, 11-13 High Road, Byfleet, Surrey

PARAFFIN

Aladdin Industries Ltd, Greenford, Middlesex

Eltex, George E. Elt Ltd, Eltex Works, Bramyard Road, Worcester

P. J. Bryant, Forest Road, Fishponds, Bristol

PARAFFIN AUTOMATIC

Cooper-Walker Engineering Ltd, Woodbush, Dunbar, Scotland

SOLID FUEL

The Metallic Construction Co, Bridge Works, Alfreton Road, Kent

Greenhouse Shading/Ventilation

House and Garden Automation (see *Electric In All Forms*)

Humex (see *Electric In All Forms*)

Greenhouse Watering

CAPILLARY, MIST

House and Garden Automation (see *Electric In All Forms*)

Humex (see *Electric In All Forms*)

COMPLETE SYSTEM

British Overhead Irrigation Ltd, Home Garden Dept, Ringwood, Hampshire

VARIOUS

Camplex Products (see *Electric In All Forms*)

VARIOUS AUTOMATIC SYSTEMS

Access Frames, Crick, Rugby

Propagators

Access Frames, Crick, Rugby

Camplex Products (see *Electric In All Forms*)

House and Garden Automation (see *Electric In All Forms*)

Humex (see *Electric In All Forms*)

Warrick Propagators, Dependable Plastics Ltd, Chigwell Row, Essex

Thermometers

Diplex Ltd, Diplex Building, PO Box 172, Verulam Passage, Station Road, Watford WD1 1XB, Herts

House and Garden Automation (see *Electric In All Forms*)

Humex (see *Electric In All Forms*)

Sheds

VERY STRONG DESIGNS

Banbury Buildings Holdings Ltd (see *Summerhouses*)

F. Pratten & Co Ltd (see *Summerhouses*)

Robert H. Hall & Co (Kent) Ltd (see *Summerhouses*)

T. Bath & Co Ltd (see *Summerhouses*)

Worth Buildings Ltd (see *Greenhouses*)

Shed Fittings

TOOL RACK

Hall & Goulding Ltd, Shrimpney Road, Bognor Regis, Sussex

WORK BENCH

Robert H. Hall & Co (Kent) Ltd (see *Summerhouses*)

Bits and Pieces

ANDY GLOVES

Tedson Thornley & Co Ltd, Rochdale, Lancs

COMPOST BIN

Hall & Goulding Ltd (see *Shed Fittings*)

GLOVES, SHOES, KNEELING STOOL

E. J. Woodman & Sons Ltd (see *Carrying*)

INCINERATOR

Valor-Ironcrete Ltd, Ironcrete Works, Dorking, Surrey

LADDERS

Lloyds Ladders Ltd, Union Lane, Droitwich

Index

Numbers in italic indicate plates